AN IDENTIFICATION
GUIDE TO
DOG
BREEDS

DON HARPER

GALLERY BOOKS
An imprint of W.H. Smith Publishers Inc.
112 Madison Avenue
New York, New York 10016

A QUINTET BOOK

Produced for
GALLERY BOOKS
an imprint of W. H. Smith Publishers, Inc.
112 Madison Avenue
New York, New York 10016

ISBN 0–8317–4818–4

This book was designed and produced by
Quintet Publishing Limited
6 Blundell Street
London N7 9BH

Creative Director: *Terry Jeavons*
Designer: *Wayne Blades*
Project Editors: *Damian Thompson, David
Barraclough*
Editor: *Lesley M. Young*
Illustrators: *Paul Hart, Helen Jones, Kate Harrison*
Photographer: *Marc Henrie*

Typeset in Great Britain by
Central Southern Typesetters, Eastbourne
Manufactured in Hong Kong by Regent Publishing
Services Limited
Printed in Singapore by Tien Wah Press (Pte) Ltd.

CONTENTS

INTRODUCTION

Human contact with dogs as companion animals began at least 12,000 years ago. Scientific studies suggest that all today's breeds are descended from grey wolves (*Canis lupus*), and bearing in mind that this species of wolf was formerly the most widely distributed of all mammals in the northern hemisphere, it seems likely that domestication began in several places, rather than at one single locality.

These early ancestors of today's dogs were probably used for herding purposes once it was realized that they could be trained for this task. In appearance, they would certainly have been similar to the wolf but, as a result of selective breeding, differences in size soon became apparent. The grey wolf itself varies greatly in size across its wide range. Large individuals from Alaska may weigh 177 lb (80 kg), whereas the race that lives in the Asiatic steppes can be as small as 27 lb (12 kg).

By 9,000 years ago, in what is now the United States of America, a clear divergence in the size of dogs was already evident. Remains uncovered in the Beaverhead Mountains of eastern-central Idaho have revealed both a dog similar in size to today's retrievers, and a smaller version, which probably resembled a Beagle.

This trend was to continue, and as society became more stable, so dogs of different sizes were developed for specific purposes. The larger forms were used as guardians of property, while other, smaller types continued in their traditional role of herding livestock. In the Orient these distinctions arose at an early stage in Tibet. Ultimately, the descendants of these dogs, such as the Tibetan Mastiff and Tibetan Spaniel, have become known in the West within the last century or so, although they have a much older ancestry, possibly dating back a thousand years or more.

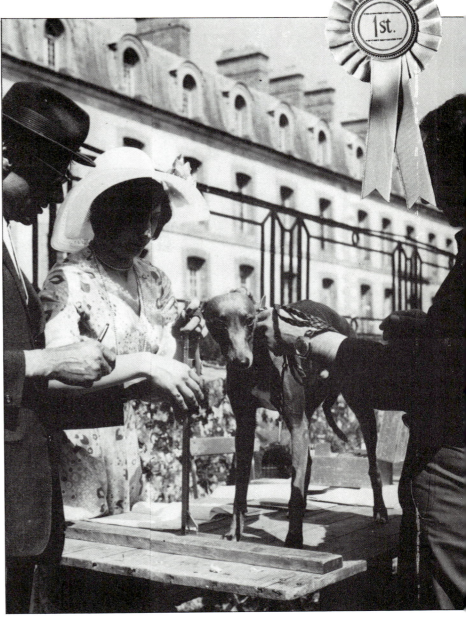

THE DEVELOPMENT OF THE PURE-BRED DOG

Localized forms obviously tended to evolve into dogs of recognizable type, although they were not breeds in the sense that we understand the term today. These dogs were bred for particular purposes rather than to conform as closely as possible to a prescribed ideal form in terms of their appearance, as pure-bred dogs are today. Interest in this field arose largely during Victorian times, when 'fancying', or the selective breeding of livestock for particular features, became highly fashionable. This was coupled to the rise of dog shows, where the various breeds were paraded and judged, with prizes being given to the winners in each category.

The most famous dog show in the world, organized by Charles Cruft, began in 1890. Originally, this had started as a show for the terrier breeds, which were extremely popular in Victorian England, but soon it began to cater for other breeds as well. Indeed, Queen Victoria herself entered some of her Pomeranians in 1891, and this royal link with dogs has continued right through to the present day.

The foundation of the Kennel Club in Great Britain, which became the governing body in the canine world, took place in 1873. This was to prove the major influence in the development of pure-bred dogs: from its inception, it began to establish stud books for the various breeds. The Kennel Club was also instrumental in establishing the standards against which the various breeds are judged. Once the Kennel Club had defined the required characteristics of the different breeds, it became possible for breeders to assess their dogs against the 'ideal' for their breed, as laid down in the standards.

Since those early years, various modifications to the individual standards have been made, and dog breeding has become much more international. As a result, many new breeds have become available, and the Kennel Club has helped to nurture their development in Britain, in conjunction with the breeders themselves and the breed societies.

The influence of the Kennel Club has also spread far afield. In the United States, the American Kennel Club was established during 1884, on similar lines to its British equivalent, and a Canadian counterpart was set up four years later. Today, similar organiziations are to be found in many countries throughout the world where dog showing is popular.

CHOOSING A BREED

During recent years, there has been growing concern about the temperament of some of the breeds, with Rottweilers in particular gaining a bad reputation in the media for their ferocity. When selecting a pure-bred dog, you must always consider its ancestry. Inherited traits established over many generations will still influence the behaviour of the breed today. The Rottweiler has a long history as a brave and powerful guard dog, and has obviously retained some potentially aggressive traits within its personality.

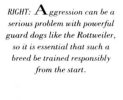

RIGHT: **A***ggression can be a serious problem with powerful guard dogs like the Rottweiler, so it is essential that such a breed be trained responsibly from the start.*

Aside from providing us with companionship, dogs are still used for various working purposes. The Rottweiler is sometimes employed as a police dog, emphasizing the responsive and intelligent side of its nature. Other dogs, bred primarily for hunting purposes, are much harder to train successfully. Hounds such as the Afghan will prove far less amenable in this regard when compared to other sporting dogs, such as members of the retriever group. Throughout their existence, the

retriever breeds have worked closely alongside their owners. It is no coincidence that while still fulfilling their traditional role as gundogs, retrievers are also now used as guide dogs for the blind and for people who are hard of hearing. Their excellent scenting abilities mean that they can also be trained successfully to detect drugs and explosives.

Working sheepdogs can still be found throughout the world and they make popular companions, although these dogs may sometimes become rather bored and frustrated in urban surroundings. It is important to consider the individual needs of the breed, together with your own personal surroundings, before making any decision about obtaining a dog. Sadly, too many people base their choice simply on a breed's appearance, without considering its evolution.

While it is obvious that a large dog requires more space, and will prove more costly to feed than a smaller breed, other factors, such as the dog's temperament and ease of training are likely to be more relevant to the relationship between dog and owner, and, ultimately, to the enjoyment of ownership. Other factors to consider when choosing a breed are the coat care required – the smooth-coated breeds such as the Greyhound being the least demanding in this regard – and, possibly, its lifespan. As a rough guide, the large breeds, such as the Irish Wolfhound, may live for

pleasure as pets, but beware of any individuals with a known physical deformity. These could prove a source of worry and trouble, not to mention veterinary expense, in later life.

Although it is sometimes claimed that cross-bred (mongrel) puppies are healthier than their pure-bred counterparts, there is no real truth in this assertion. They are equally susceptible to diseases such as distemper and the various parasites that may afflict dogs. There is possibly a greater risk, however, that pure-bred dogs may suffer from certain congenital weaknesses such as hip dysplasia (HD) or progressive retinal atrophy (PRA). Responsible breeders will have their breeding stock screened for these particular conditions, thus minimizing the risk of the problem occurring later in their offspring.

less than a decade, whereas many of the smaller dogs will remain active well into their teens.

The cost of a pedigree dog is influenced by several factors. The relative scarcity of a breed will have a direct impact on its price, as under these circumstances demand will probably outstrip supply and there may well be a waiting list for puppies. The quality of both the bloodline, measured in terms of show performance, and the potential of the individual puppies themselves will also influence the price asked by the breeder. If you are looking simply for a pet dog, rather than a good show specimen, the cost should be correspondingly lower.

Breeders invariably have some surplus puppies that, possibly because of faults in their markings for example, will not do well in the show ring. Such dogs will invariably settle down and give great

BELOW: **P***oodle puppies at 2 days old*

LEFT: **G***uide dogs for the blind, or 'seeing eyes' as they are called in the United States, must rank as the most valuable group of trained dogs.*

CHOOSING AN INDIVIDUAL DOG

RIGHT: **A** *careful veterinary examination is essential before vaccinating a young puppy.*

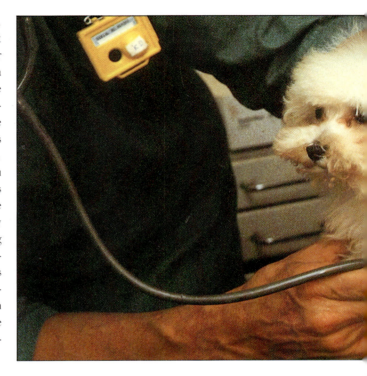

Having decided on a particular breed, you can then track down puppies without too much difficulty in most cases. Your veterinarian may be able to suggest a breeder within your locality, and there are also directories which list breeders of pedigree dogs, often on a regional basis. The various dog magazines and newspapers may also be a useful source of reference. It will obviously make life easier if you obtain your puppy as close to home as possible, although, particularly if you are looking for a potential show dog, you may want to see several litters before taking any decision, and this may entail travelling further afield. In the United States especially, a good range of pedigree puppies are available from pet stores, although you will obviously not have the advantage of seeing their parents or home surroundings if you buy from such a source.

RIGHT: **M** *any infectious diseases may cause severe dehydration owing to persistent vomiting and diarrhoea. To replace the fluid an intravenous drip is required.*

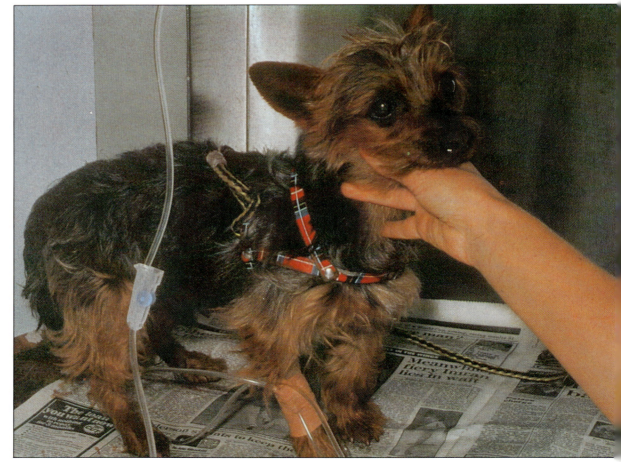

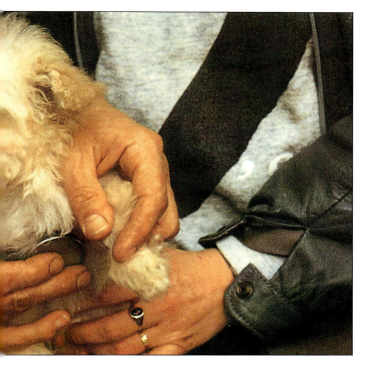

It is obviously vital to select a healthy puppy, and if you are at all concerned, especially when considering a puppy in a pet store, it would be best to delay your purchase. Puppies are normally lively, but remember that they will sleep for longer than adult dogs. Always watch them running about, as this will reveal any trace of lameness. The puppy's skin should feel quite loose when you handle it, and, over all, it ought to be relatively plump.

There should be no trace of either fleas or lice on the coat. If the pup is distinctly pot-bellied, this tends to be indicative of a heavy burden of intestinal parasites. When you are feeling around in this area, locate the remains of the umbilicus, in the mid-line of the body. In a few cases, a hernia may have occurred during the birth process, creating a swelling that might need to be corrected by surgery later.

The puppy's motions should appear firm, although, occasionally, following deworming, an outbreak of diarrhoea may result. Even so, view any puppies with diarrhoea cautiously, as this could be evidence of a more serious affliction. In any event, always make an appointment to take a newly acquired puppy to a veterinarian at an early opportunity, both for a health check and to discuss the necessary schedule of vaccinations. You must also sort out the paperwork regarding the transfer of ownership of the puppy to you, which will mean notifying the registration authority in the country concerned. The breeder should be able to advise you if you have any doubts about this procedure.

LEFT: **A** *Cavalier King Charles Spaniel bitch suckles her three puppies.*

THE PLAN OF THIS BOOK

For ease of reference over the following pages, the various breeds here have been grouped on the basis of their size. It is hoped that this will provide a useful starting point, especially for novice owners, who may be unfamiliar with the wide variety of breeds that are available in the different categories.

Nevertheless, it is important to bear in mind that simply because a dog is large, this does not necessarily mean it will prove more active in domestic surroundings than a smaller breed. Indeed, whereas a Greyhound, for example, ranks amongst the most athletic of dogs, it proves quite sedentary within the home. Some smaller breeds, such as the Beagle, may actually be more frenetic here.

THE PANELS

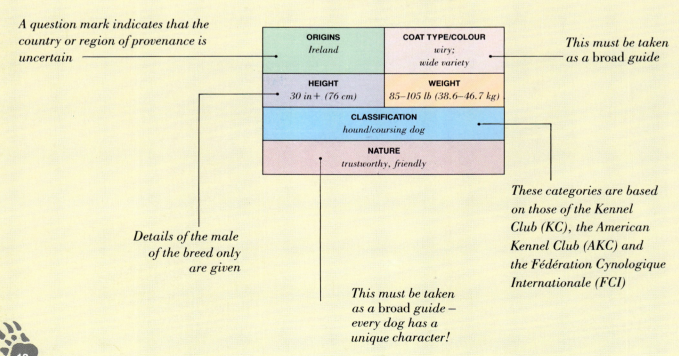

A question mark indicates that the country or region of provenance is uncertain

ORIGINS	COAT TYPE/COLOUR
Ireland	*wiry; wide variety*

HEIGHT	WEIGHT
30 in + (76 cm)	*85–105 lb (38.6–46.7 kg)*

CLASSIFICATION
hound/coursing dog

NATURE
trustworthy, friendly

This must be taken as a broad guide

Details of the male of the breed only are given

These categories are based on those of the Kennel Club (KC), the American Kennel Club (AKC) and the Fédération Cynologique Internationale (FCI)

This must be taken as a broad guide – every dog has a unique character!

1
MINIATURE BREEDS

SMALL DOGS UP TO 12 in (30 cm)

This group of small breeds, measuring up to 12 in (30 cm) in height at the shoulder, includes not only the popular toy breeds, such as the Chihuahua, but also many of the traditional working breeds, such as the Norfolk Terrier. There is thus a wide choice within this category, reflecting the diverse ancestries of these dogs.

AFFENPINSCHER

ORIGINS	COAT TYPE/COLOUR
Germany	wiry, longish; black
HEIGHT	**WEIGHT**
9½–11 in (24–28 cm)	6½–9 lb (2.9–4 kg)
CLASSIFICATION	
toy/companion	
NATURE	
lively, loyal, sometimes stubborn	

As its name suggests, this breed originated in Australia, in tandem with its close relative, simply known as the Australian Terrier. Both breeds are descended from imported British terriers, and bear an obvious similarity in appearance to the Yorkshire Terrier. In the United States, to avoid possible confusion over the names of these two terriers, they are now described as the Silky and Australian Terriers, respectively.

It is likely that the Australian Silky Terrier is the combined result of three separate British breeds which were involved in its development. The Dandie Dinmont Terrier probably contributed towards the breed's relatively long body, as well as its silky coat. Skye Terriers may also have emphasized this characteristic, while its blue coloration probably came from the Yorkshire Terrier.

The coat of the Australian Silky Terrier, which is straight and silky to the touch, is usually parted over the head and down the centre of the back. It is not as long as that of the Yorkshire Terrier, although there is a topknot on the top of the head. Today, the ears are held erect, although, formerly, drop ears were also permissible, suggesting a close relationship with the Skye Terrier.

In terms of care, the Australian Silky Terrier is probably less demanding than its appearance may suggest, daily brushing being adequate to keep its coat in top condition. It is a lively breed, but will adapt well to apartment-living, if it can have a good walk each day.

BICHON FRISÉ

ORIGINS	COAT TYPE/COLOUR
Tenerife	curly; pure white
HEIGHT	**WEIGHT**
up to 12 in (30.5 cm)	7–12 lb (3.2–5.4 kg)
CLASSIFICATION	
toy/non-sporting/companion	
NATURE	
easy to train; a good companion	

An old breed whose history dates back over 300 years, the Affenpinscher is probably descended from a combination of small wire-haired terriers and pug-like dogs. It originated in Germany and is sometimes known as the Monkey Dog, because of its facial features, which resemble those of certain primates. The bushy area of hair above the mouth, and the flattish nose, have led the French to refer to this breed less flatteringly as the *Diabletin Moustache* – the moustached little devil.

In terms of personality, however, the Affenpinscher has all the best qualities of the terrier breeds. These little dogs are lively, loyal and affectionate, although they may prove stubborn on occasions. The coat is wiry in texture and relatively long, but grooming is quite straightforward, a daily brushing usually proving adequate. The preferred coloration for the coat is black, but grey, black and tan, and red individuals may be encountered on occasion as well.

Affenpinschers require a daily walk, although this need not be a lengthy period of exercise. They also enjoy a run off the leash in suitably safe surroundings. The breed was first recognized by the American Kennel Club in 1936, and then by the Kennel Club in Great Britain during 1980.

In the Affenpinscher, the lower jaw may be slightly longer than the upper; although this undershot arrangement is often considered a fault in other breeds, it is not regarded as a weakness in this case.

AUSTRALIAN SILKY TERRIER (SILKY TERRIER)

ORIGINS	COAT TYPE/COLOUR
Australia	*silky; bluish and tan*
HEIGHT	**WEIGHT**
9 in (23 cm)	*8–10 lb (3.6–4.5 kg)*
CLASSIFICATION	
toy/terrier	
NATURE	
lively, adaptable	

The cuddly Bichon Frisé is believed to have originated in Tenerife, one of the Canary Islands off the west coast of Africa. Its ancestors were brought to Europe over 400 years ago, and became especially popular among members of the Spanish and French aristocracy. Support for the breed declined during the nineteenth century, however, and it became associated with organ-grinders, who relied on its attractive appearance to induce generous support from onlookers.

In the circus ring, its intelligence endeared it to another audience, but it was to be the First World War that began the welcome rise in popularity of these dogs. Soldiers returning home with the Bichons meant that attention became focused on the breed in Britain. A standard was first established in France in 1933, and the breed was exported to the United States by a Monsieur Picault and his wife in 1956.

The coat colour of the Bichon Frisé is pure white, with the hairs being naturally curly. Unfortunately, to retain the immaculate appearance of these little dogs, a considerable amount of time must be devoted to grooming. Its white coat can become muddy on even a short walk. In such cases, it is best to let the mud dry and then brush it out of the coat, rather than washing the legs frequently. It is usual for puppies to have a less elaborate coat than older dogs. The Bichon Frisé should prove a relatively easy breed to train and makes a good companion.

BORDER TERRIER

ORIGINS	COAT TYPE/COLOUR
Cheviot Hills, England	*short; wide variety*

HEIGHT	WEIGHT
10 in (25 cm)	*13–15½ lb (5.9–7 kg)*

CLASSIFICATION	
terrier	

NATURE	
great stamina; responsive to training	

One of a number of localized Scottish breeds of terrier that have become known to dog-lovers throughout the world, the Cairn's history dates back over 500 years. It evolved in the west of the country and also on the Isle of Skye, whence the Skye Terrier also originated. Indeed, when they were first exhibited in 1909, Cairns were described as Short-haired Skye Terriers, but objections from Skye breeders led to the adoption of their current name. Cairn terriers, so-called after the Gaelic word for a pyramid of stones, would often hunt vermin in the vicinity of such stones, and this name now has universal acceptance. The Cairn was introduced in the United States in 1913.

These terriers are very even-tempered and affectionate, making them an ideal choice for a home where there are children. They will readily take part in ball-games and other family activities. Their shaggy coat provides adequate protection against the elements. If the opportunity presents itself, Cairn Terriers will instinctively hunt vermin – still an advantageous trait, especially in rural areas.

One possible drawback of their tendency to go to ground is their desire to dig, and they may have to be taught not to use flowerbeds for this purpose. However, this is a small problem that can usually be overcome without difficulty. You can purchase special chemical deterrents for this purpose from pet shops; these simply need to be applied around the flowerbeds.

CHIHUAHUA

ORIGINS	COAT TYPE/COLOUR
Mexico	*smooth, long; creamy, bluish*

HEIGHT	WEIGHT
6–9 in (15–23 cm)	*2–6 lb (0.9–2.7 kg)*

CLASSIFICATION	
toy/companion	

NATURE	
very loyal; dislikes cold; a finnicky eater	

riginating in the Cheviot Hills that separate England from Scotland, the Border Terrier is the smallest of the working terrier breeds. It was first known as the Reedwater Terrier, a localized name, before being recognized under its present name in 1880. A tough and hardy breed, the Border was used originally to drive foxes from their earths. Indeed, Border Terriers are still kept for working purposes in their homeland today, although their precise ancestry now appears unknown. They are probably related to other terriers from this region, such as the Lakeland and Dandie Dinmont breeds. They probably acquired the name of Border Terrier as a result of working alongside the Border Foxhounds. In spite of their size, these terriers have the tremendous stamina required for hunting in this terrain, accompanying riders on horseback.

For this reason, you should only acquire one of these terriers if you can give it a long walk on a regular daily basis. Their short coats are easy to keep in good condition, and a range of colours, from wheaten to red and both blue and tan and grizzle and tan are all permissible for show purposes. The coat does not need stripping to remove dead hair, and possibly only a brief trim will be required if you wish to show a Border Terrier. They have probably altered less in appearance down the years than other terrier breeds, and are particularly responsive to training.

CAIRN TERRIER

ORIGINS	COAT TYPE/COLOUR
West Scotland Isle of Skye	*rough, double-layered; wide variety*
HEIGHT	**WEIGHT**
12 in (30.5 cm)	*14 lb (6.4 kg)*
CLASSIFICATION	
terrier	
NATURE	
affectionate; ideal for children	

amed after the Mexican state where they were first obtained, these dogs are the likely descendants of a very old breed, known as the Techichi, which was kept here by the Toltec Indians as far back as the ninth century AD.

Recognized by the American Kennel Club in 1904, the original Chihuahuas were smooth-coated, but through crossing these with other dog breeds it was possible for breeders in the United States to produce long-coated forms. Obviously, these dogs require more grooming to keep their coats in top condition.

Chihuahuas are very loyal by nature, and live well in reasonably confined surroundings, although they do have quite a penetrating and persistent bark for their size. They dislike the cold, and are surprisingly social by nature, so if you find that you have to be out at times, consider a companion for your dog. This can also help to overcome the rather finicky eating habits of some Chihuahuas, as will offering small quantities of food three or four times during the day.

This is not a breed recommended for children as Chihuahuas can prove short-tempered and may then snap, while they can also be fatally injured by a blow on the head. Instead of having a solid casing to the skull, as is normal, Chihuahuas generally have an opening here, known as the molera, like that of a new-born human baby. This never ossifies, leaving the brain vulnerable as a result.

DACHSHUND

ORIGINS	COAT TYPE/COLOUR
Germany	*smooth/wiry;* *black and amber*

HEIGHT	WEIGHT
5–9 in (12.5–23 cm)	*18 lb (8.2 kg)*

CLASSIFICATION
hound/dachshund

NATURE
loyal; susceptible to back injury

A number of different types of Dachshund are now recognized, descended from short-legged hunting dogs that have been popular since the Middle Ages in parts of Germany. Here they were used primarily for badger-hunting, with the traditional form of the Dachshund, or Teckel as it is better known in its homeland, being the standard short-haired form. Aside from their appearance, however, it is also generally accepted that there is a difference in temperament between these lively dogs and the somewhat shyer Long-haired Dachshund, which will require more grooming. The Wire-haired Dachshund, produced by crosses involving the Dandie Dinmont Terrier and other similar breeds, is the third member of this group. Selective breeding has meant that there are now miniature versions of all three types of Dachshund as well.

As companions, Dachshunds prove loyal to their owners, and possess a bark suggestive of a larger dog. Their elongated body shape, which has led to them being nicknamed 'sausage dogs', has made them susceptible to inter-vertebral disc problems, particularly if they are overweight. As a rough guide, like most of the other dogs covered in this section, they need about half a can of standard complete dog food (7 oz/200 g), with a similar volume of biscuit meal, which can be measured out using a clean can. As a further precaution against disc injuries, take pains to discourage these dogs from running up the stairs or jumping up onto furniture.

DANDIE DINMONT TERRIER

ORIGINS	COAT TYPE/COLOUR
the border counties, Great Britain	longish; mustard/pepper
HEIGHT	**WEIGHT**
8–11 in (20.5–28 cm)	18 lb (8.2 kg)
CLASSIFICATION	
terrier	
NATURE	
devoted, but can be stubborn	

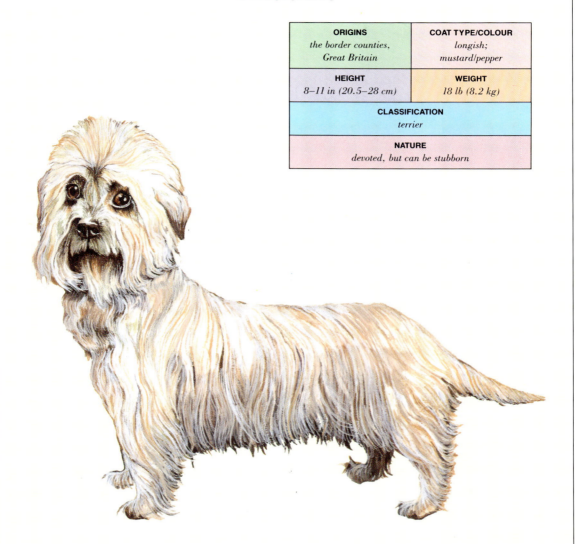

One of the less common terrier breeds today, the Dandie Dinmont is another that emerged from the border counties separating England and Scotland. It became famous through the writings of Sir Walter Scott, being named after a farmer who featured in his novel *Guy Mannering*. The unmistakable appearance of these terriers results from the top-knot of hair on their heads, coupled with their relatively long ears. They were originally used to hunt badgers and otters. Dandie Dinmonts tend to become devoted to their owners, but are likely to remain reserved with strangers. Unfortunately, they do have a stubborn side to their nature, and this can make training a somewhat more difficult procedure than with other terriers.

The unusual texture of the coat results from a combination of both hard and soft hairs. Both a brush and a comb are needed for grooming purposes. The hair must be plucked to prevent it becoming too long and faded. For show purposes, Dandie Dinmont Terriers are divided into two groups in terms of coloration. Those that are termed mustard are of a more yellowish tone, varying from reddish-brown to pale fawn, whereas peppers can range from a light shade of silvery-grey through to bluish-black. Coloration is paler on the underside of the body, and the hair is usually softer here as well. Although this breed rarely wins top awards in mixed company, it is an attractive addition to any show.

FRENCH BULLDOG

ORIGINS *United States*	COAT TYPE/COLOUR *smooth; dark brown and white*
HEIGHT *12 in (30.5 cm)*	WEIGHT *28 lb (12.7 kg)*
CLASSIFICATION *utility/companion/sporting*	
NATURE *intelligent, quiet; requires little exercise*	

Better known in the United States as the Brussels Griffon, these toy dogs are thought to be descended from the Affenpinscher. Various subdivisions of the breed are recognized in Europe, based essentially on the colour of the coat. The Griffon Bruxellois is, by definition, pure red in Europe, whereas the Griffin Belge is black, or a combination of black and tan. The third form, produced by cross-breeding with the Pug is the Brabançon, distinguishable by virtue of its smooth, short coat.

While even the most devoted admirer of these dogs would not claim that they were particularly attractive in appearance, they have much in their favour in terms of temperament. The Griffon Bruxellois is a responsive and affectionate breed, which is quite easy to train and settles well in fairly urbanized surroundings. They used to be kept as stable dogs bred for killing vermin, but soon progressed to riding on the seat at the front of horse-drawn cabs, next to the cabbie. Their appealing natures would doubtless have endeared them to passengers. The Griffon Bruxellois became known in Britain just before the turn of the century, and reached the United States for the first time soon afterwards. They are easy in terms of care, although the rough-coated varieties will need to be stripped about twice a year. This can be carried out easily in a grooming parlour.

JAPANESE CHIN

ORIGINS *China*	COAT TYPE/COLOUR *silky; black (or red) and white*
HEIGHT *9 in max (23 cm)*	WEIGHT *7 lb (3.2 kg)*
CLASSIFICATION *toy/companion*	
NATURE *bright and lively*	

In the middle of the nineteenth century, bull-dogs were among the most popular dogs in England, especially in urban areas. Various strains were available and among these were miniature forms, which appear to have been common in the Midlands. These appealed particularly to French breeders and a number were in all likelihood exported to France during this period.

From France these dogs were taken to the United States. While European breeders tended to favour the floppy or 'rose' ear characteristic of the Bulldog itself, American enthusiasts preferred to breed these smaller bulldogs with upright, bat-type ears. These dogs were brought to England about 1900, and a dispute promptly broke out over their name because it was felt in some quarters that the term 'bull-dog' could only be associated with a British breed.

Agreement was finally reached, however, and today the French Bulldog is highly appreciated both as a pet and by breeders. Its facial changes are less extreme than those presently associated with the Bulldog. It does not snuffle to the same extent, nor is it as susceptible to heat exhaustion. Even so, it is not a great lover of exercise, and will be content with a short walk each day, broken by a brief period off the leash. You may need to watch for occasional signs of localized infection in its facial creases, but this can be dealt with effectively through treatment by your veterinarian.

GRIFFON BRUXELLOIS (BRUSSELS GRIFFON)

ORIGINS	COAT TYPE/COLOUR
Belgium/Germany	*shaggy; pure red*
HEIGHT	**WEIGHT**
7 in max (18 cm)	*5–11 lb (2.3–5 kg)*
CLASSIFICATION	
toy/companion	
NATURE	
sensitive, easy to train, intelligent	

In spite of its name, the Japanese Chin was first bred in China, and is one of the oldest of all toy breeds. It is thought that similar dogs were brought to Japan about AD 520 by Buddhist monks emigrating from China. In terms of appearance, the Japanese Chin has similarities to both the Pekingese and the Pug, and may share a common ancestry with them. They were accorded divine status by one Japanese emperor, and kept exclusively by members of the nobility. It is believed that the first pair of these dogs released from Japan to the West was given to one Commodore Perry in 1853, in return for establishing trade links with Japan. Queen Victoria, who was a keen dog-lover herself, soon acquired the breed, and Japanese Chins were first seen in the United States in 1882.

Although some of the original stock did not settle well after the long journey by sea from Japan, today's examples of the breed are hardy and long-lived dogs. They have an attractive silky coat, which can only be kept in top condition by careful grooming every day with a bristle brush. The Japanese Chin is either black and white or red and white, with the red in this case being variable and encompassing shades of lemon, orange, brindle and sable. An even distribution of the coloured areas across the body is deemed preferable, with the tail curling down over the back. Puppies tend to have a less profuse coat than adults.

KING CHARLES SPANIEL
(ENGLISH TOY SPANIEL)

ORIGINS	COAT TYPE/COLOUR
England	*smooth, long; wide variety*

HEIGHT	WEIGHT
10 in (25 cm)	*8–14 lb (3.6–6.4 kg)*

CLASSIFICATION
toy/companion

NATURE
friendly, adaptable; requires careful grooming

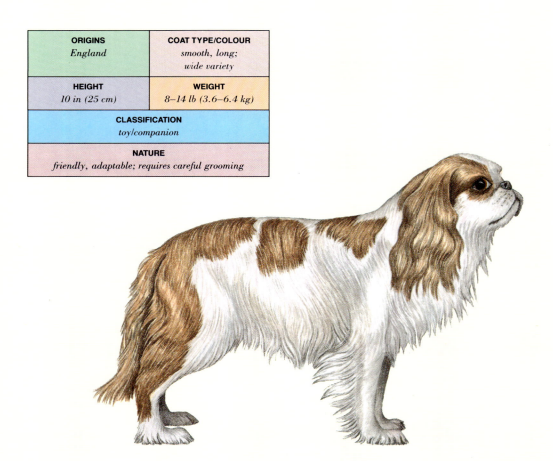

Although closely related to the Cavalier King Charles Spaniel (see page 38), this particular breed is significantly smaller, and, to avoid confusion, is better known in the United States as the English Toy Spaniel. These dogs were apparently great favourites of King Charles II (1660–85), who used to exercise his pets personally in St James's Park in London. Four distinct varieties are recognized today, on the basis of their coloration, the traditional form being black and tan. The others are the Prince Charles, which is tri-coloured, the Ruby, which is chestnut-red, and the Blenheim, a combination of ruby and white markings, initially bred by the First Duke of Marlborough and named after his palace.

The nose of this breed is much shorter than that of the Cavalier, and the flattened face may make the prominent eyes more prone to injury as a result. You will need to check the ears regularly in this breed, as they are both pendulous and heavy. As a consequence, infections can develop quite easily within the ear canal, with persistent scratching being an early sign of irritation. Seek veterinary assistance without delay, as some infections of this type can be difficult to cure successfully, especially if treatment is delayed.

These spaniels, which vary considerably in size, are usually friendly dogs and should settle well in the company of other pets, notably cats, without problems. You must be prepared to groom the coat each day, and the eyes may also benefit from being wiped over at the corners with moist cotton wool, to remove any build-up of dirt.

NORFOLK AND NORWICH TERRIERS

ORIGINS	COAT TYPE/COLOUR
East Anglia, England	shaggy; tan
HEIGHT	**WEIGHT**
10 in (25 cm)	10–12 lb (4.5–5.4 kg)
CLASSIFICATION	
terrier	
NATURE	
hardy and loyal	

In the eastern counties of England, a breed of hunting terrier that was rather similar to the Border Terrier in many ways, including coloration, was bred during the early 1800s. However, it was only towards the end of the nineteenth century that these terriers started to attract attention, becoming popular with students at Cambridge University. Subsequent crosses involving Glen of Imaal Terriers, Dandie Dinmonts and others saw the emergence of the type of dog that has since become known as the Norfolk Terrier.

These terriers were taken to the United States at an early stage in their history, and used in a traditional manner to drive out a fox that had gone to earth. Here they were originally known as Jones Terriers. However, in 1964 a decision was taken by the Kennel Club in Great Britain,

which split the breed on the basis of ear carriage, and the American Kennel Club also agreed to follow this precedent in 1979. Now Norfolk Terriers are deemed to have folded ears in both countries, whereas Norwich Terriers have ears that are held erect.

In terms of temperament, neither breed is quarrelsome by nature, although they are strong, active dogs for their size. They are best kept in fairly rural surroundings, where they can obtain more exercise. Their coat is wiry to the touch and needs little grooming. The dense thickness of the undercoat provides good insulation, even against water. Norfolk and Norwich Terriers show a loyal and trustworthy nature towards people whom they know well, and settle happily in a home with children. They should not be considered as typical toy dogs.

PAPILLON AND PHALENE

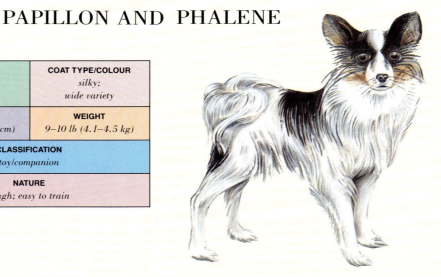

ORIGINS	COAT TYPE/COLOUR
?Spain	*silky;* *wide variety*
HEIGHT	**WEIGHT**
8–11 in (20.5–28 cm)	*9–10 lb (4.1–4.5 kg)*
CLASSIFICATION	
toy/companion	
NATURE	
tough; easy to train	

Another of the ancient Oriental breeds, whose ancestry can be traced back to the T'ang dynasty, about 1,200 years ago, the Pekingese was finally brought to Europe for the first time in 1860, following the seizure of Peking by British troops. Prior to this, these dogs had been closely associated with the Chinese imperial court, and could only be kept by the nobility. They were known as sleeve dogs, because their small size enabled them to be carried within the flowing robes of the emperor.

One of the first Pekingese obtained from China was presented to Queen Victoria in England, and this helped to gain the breed immediate popularity. These small dogs are available in a wide range of colours and colour combinations, all of which are acceptable for show purposes except for liver and albino. They enjoy being lavished with affection, as befits their royal ancestry, but they are quite hardy little dogs as well.

Take care when exercising them during periods of hot weather, as Pekingese can suffer from heat stroke. Their prominent eyes are also vulnerable to injury, and they should certainly be discouraged from running through undergrowth once off the leash. You must be prepared to groom the flowing coat every day in order to prevent it from becoming tangled. The Pekingese is an ideal breed for people who are at home on their own throughout the day, as it will form a strong bond with its owner. Left alone to their own devices for long, however, the intelligent and mischievous side to their nature will soon become apparent, and they are likely to prove destructive.

POMERANIAN

ORIGINS	COAT TYPE/COLOUR
Germany	*flowing;* *wide variety*
HEIGHT	**WEIGHT**
12 in (30.5 cm)	*4–4½ lb (1.8–2 kg)*
CLASSIFICATION	
toy/companion	
NATURE	
sturdy, alert, good-tempered	

The name of this breed refers to the positioning and shape of its ears, and is derived from the French word *Papillon* meaning butterfly. The raised ears are said to resemble a butterfly's wings, while in the case of the closely related continental toy spaniel, known as the Phalene, they hang downwards over the sides of the head.

The precise origins of these dogs are unclear, although, bearing in mind their popularity among the nobility of mainland Europe during the seventeenth century, crosses involving the Bichon Frise and small spaniels may have contributed to their ancestry. The dainty movements of the Papillon belie its robust constitution. Whereas some toy breeds, such as the Chihuahua, may encounter difficulties when whelping, this type of problem is distinctly uncommon in the Papillon. They are easy dogs to care for, and will live quite happily in an apartment, if they can have daily exercise.

Papillons are intelligent and invariably keen to please their owners, which in turn makes them relatively easy dogs to train successfully. However, you will need to ensure that they do not become too demanding and possessive, which can be a fault associated with the breed. Try to involve other members of the family as much as possible in the dog's care, so as to prevent the occurrence of this problem. Both the Papillon and the Phalene have been bred in a wide range of colours, with only liver and white outlawed for show purposes, so you should find a good choice of colours available if you decide to purchase a puppy.

PEKINGESE

ORIGINS		COAT TYPE/COLOUR	
China		*flowing; wide variety*	
HEIGHT		**WEIGHT**	
6–9 in (15–23 cm)		*11 lb (5 kg)*	
CLASSIFICATION			
toy/companion			
NATURE			
affectionate, stubborn, pompous			

This is the smallest member of the group of spitz dogs, distinguished by their curly tails and upright ears. It appears to have been developed in the German province of Pomerania, and attracted the attention of Queen Victoria. She exhibited the breed at the Crufts Show of 1891, and this immediately led to an upsurge of interest in these dogs. Originally, Pomeranians were much larger than they are today, weighing as much as 30 lb (13.6 kg), but now members of this breed are lighter than 8 lb (3.6 kg). Nevertheless, they have retained the typical temperament of a spitz dog, being lively and loyal, and generally prove easy to train. Pomeranians are available in a wide range of colours, and will live quite contentedly in a home where there is a small garden, with a park in the neighbourhood for more prolonged periods of exercise.

Grooming is more time consuming than with some breeds, as the Pomeranian has a dense undercoat and a long, straight outer coat. Trimming will also be necessary on occasion, to ensure that the coat remains immaculate. They are very alert dogs and will indicate the presence of strangers by yapping loudly. Although this can be advantageous under certain circumstances, you may need to dissuade a Pomeranian from barking unnecessarily at the slightest sound. Nevertheless, as small guard dogs they can give great reassurance, especially to elderly owners who are living on their own.

POODLE: TOY

ORIGINS	COAT TYPE/COLOUR
Germany	*curly, shaggy; wide variety*
HEIGHT	**WEIGHT**
under 11 in (28 cm)	*15 lb (6.8 kg)*
CLASSIFICATION	
utility/toy/companion	
NATURE	
intelligent, active, friendly	

It is believed that the ancestors of this breed were obtained in China by the Dutch East India Company, who brought these dogs back to Holland. Here they obtained royal patronage and were adopted as the symbol of the House of Orange. They were brought to Britain when William of Orange became King of England in 1689. This is another breed whose face is said to resemble that of a monkey, in this case a marmoset. These small New World primates were popular pets during the eighteenth century, and were themselves referred to as 'pugs' for a period, the name then being transferred to the dogs.

With its thick-set appearance and wrinkled face, the Pug would seem to be a miniature mastiff. It is an energetic breed, with a matching appetite, and if spoilt it will soon become obese. This will almost certainly shorten its lifespan, and will worsen any tendency towards difficulty in breathing resulting from the compact face of the breed. Exercise during the warmest part of the day is inadvisable, particularly in hot climates.

Pugs become loyal companions and are easy to care for, their short coat needing only regular grooming to remain in good condition. You can monitor the weight of a Pug quite easily, by holding it in your arms and weighing yourself. Then stand on the scales on your own, and subtract your own weight from the previous figure. Pugs should weigh between 14–18 lb (6.4–8.2 kg). If a dog appears to be putting on weight, not only should you review its diet, cutting back on biscuits in particular, but you must also give your pet more exercise.

SCOTTISH TERRIER

ORIGINS	COAT TYPE/COLOUR
Scotland	*shaggy; usually black*
HEIGHT	**WEIGHT**
10–11 in (25–28 cm)	*19–23 lb (8.6–10.4 kg)*
CLASSIFICATION	
terrier	
NATURE	
intelligent, active, friendly	

The Toy version of the Poodle is recognized as a separate breed, in spite of the fact that it shares a common ancestry with both the Miniature and the larger Standard Poodle (page 46). These particular dogs are descended from working stock, in spite of their often elaborate appearance, which may be more suggestive of a cosseted and delicate breed. In fact, Poodles were originally used to guard sheep, and, being descended from the Irish Water Spaniel, would also readily enter water as retrievers.

Interest in the Poodle as a lap dog meant that smaller individuals were favoured, and certainly the Toy form appears to have been established by the eighteenth century, according to contemporary Spanish portraits. Poodles do not moult their hair in a similar way to other breeds, and, certainly for show purposes, coat care is very time-consuming. In the case of a pet dog, however, this can be carried out at a grooming parlour. Ask the breeder for a recommendation, or, alternatively, you can contact a professional groomer through the Yellow Pages.

Although show dogs have more elaborate clips, the simple lamb clip, which merely keeps the hair at an even length, can be recommended for a Poodle kept just as a companion. This will need to be carried out about every six weeks or so, and will add to the cost of keeping your dog unless you decide to undertake the task yourself. When purchasing a puppy of this breed, it is especially important to ensure that it is sound. Like some other smaller dogs, Toy Poodles can suffer from a problem affecting the knee-caps. Known as luxation of the patella, this problem can lead to lameness.

PUG

ORIGINS		COAT TYPE/COLOUR	
China		*short;* *black, oyster*	
HEIGHT		WEIGHT	
10–11 in (25–28 cm)		*14–18 lb (6.4–8.2 kg)*	
CLASSIFICATION			
toy/companion			
NATURE			
friendly; easy to care for; weight needs watching			

Known affectionately simply as the Scottie, this breed of terrier came into fashion during the middle of the last century. It was originally called the Aberdeen Terrier, after the town where the breed first became prominent. Many people assume that the Scottish Terrier is invariably black, but it is also bred in a variety of other colours, including wheaten, which is whitish-brown, and also brindle. When grooming these terriers, particular care should be given to the beard; this may even need to be washed from time to time if it becomes soiled with sloppy food.

Scottish Terriers are brave little dogs and make alert guards around the home. They are not a particularly patient breed, however, and so not ideally suited to a home where there are young children. These terriers thrive on exercise, but you will need to take care to ensure that they do not come into conflict with other dogs once they are off the leash. Scotties are perhaps best suited to rural areas where they can live largely on their own. Even so, firm training is to be recommended, in view of their naturally dominant natures. However, if you are having trouble with rodents, few dogs will prove more effective or dedicated in dealing with them.

SHIH TZU

ORIGINS	COAT TYPE/COLOUR
Tibet	*long; wide variety*
HEIGHT	**WEIGHT**
10½ in max (26.5 cm)	*10–18 lb (4.5–8.2 kg)*
CLASSIFICATION	
utility/toy/companion	
NATURE	
intelligent; requires company	

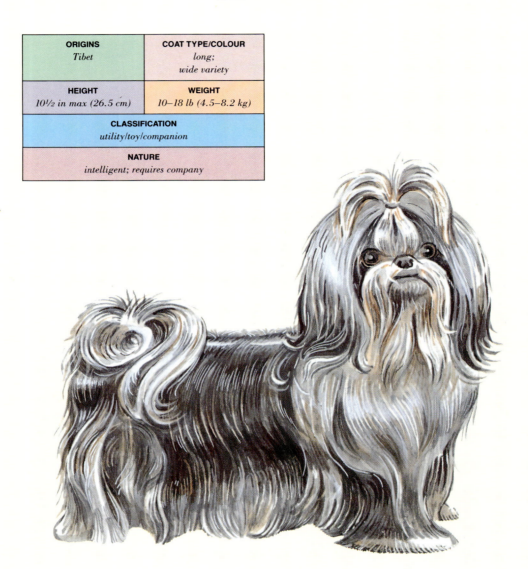

The unusual name of this breed, which is pronounced 'Shiszoo', actually means 'lion'. The Shih Tzu was originally bred in Tibet, and then developed further in China. It is closely related to both the Tibetan Terrier and the Lhasa Apso, and has become smaller in size through selective breeding. The Pekingese may also have played a part in the development of this ancient breed. It remained unknown in the West until the early years of the twentieth century, and much of today's stock can be traced back to a number of dogs obtained from China during the 1930s.

The Shih Tzu is a true companion breed, being naturally affectionate and friendly towards people of all ages. It is intelligent and will not thrive on its own, rapidly becoming bored under these circumstances. A wide range of colours has been bred, and, in view of its long coat, daily grooming is absolutely essential in all cases, otherwise the hair will become badly tangled and will then be painful to unravel. You may prefer to keep the long top-knot of hair away from the eyes by means of a bow.

You must ensure that you check the ears regularly for any signs of infection. The hair around the mouth will also have to be cleaned should it become soiled with food. Shih Tzus do not need long runs. Instead, they are perfectly content with regular short walks, and are unlikely to stray far away when off the leash.

SKYE TERRIER

ORIGINS *Isle of Skye*	COAT TYPE/COLOUR *double-layered; generally cream*
HEIGHT *10 in (25 cm)*	WEIGHT *25 lb (11.3 kg)*
CLASSIFICATION *terrier*	
NATURE *hardy; requires much exercise*	

This long-coated terrier breed was developed on the Isle of Skye off the west coast of Scotland. As befits a small breed developed for hunting animals such as foxes and badgers, it has a fearless nature. Skye Terriers are also very loyal to their owners, but are reluctant to accept strangers. This may need to be borne in mind when you are looking at adult dogs of this breed. There is a famous story concerning the devotion of one Skye Terrier called Greyfriars Bobby. After his owner's death, Bobby visited the grave every day for a decade, until he himself finally died. A statue commemorating the terrier's loyalty was subsequently erected in Greyfriars Churchyard near Edinburgh.

Puppies do not have such an elegant coat as an adult dog, but, even so, you should be prepared to spend time each day grooming it. At the same time, as with all dogs, it is a good idea to open the puppy's mouth, so that, in the future it will not resent this treatment. This is particularly important with a Skye Terrier, as this breed may be reluctant to allow a stranger such as a veterinarian to undertake this task without attempting to bite.

In spite of their rather manicured appearance, these terriers have remained hardy, working dogs. They will benefit from plenty of exercise off the leash, following up scents and investigating their surroundings. The Skye Terrier is a breed probably best suited to a rural environment, rather than an urban lifestyle. The breed has gone into decline during recent years.

WELSH CORGIS

ORIGINS *Wales*	COAT TYPE/COLOUR *short; tan,* *cream and black*
HEIGHT *10–12 in (25–30.5 cm)*	WEIGHT *24 lb (10.9 kg)*
CLASSIFICATION *working/herding*	
NATURE *intelligent; easy to train; tendency to nip*	

This breed was originally known as the Pol-talloch Terrier, being named after the area where it was first bred, in Argyllshire, Scotland. Its development here occurred by chance, when a dark-coloured terrier owned by one Colonel Malcolm was accidentally shot and killed by its owner in 1860. He then decided to breed only white terriers, and so the Westie came into existence, although, prior to this, odd white terriers had been recorded.

As with other similar breeds from this region, the West Highland White Terrier was used to hunt vermin. Its rough, wiry coat reflects its hardy ancestry, with mud soon falling off the hairs once they are dry. Regular grooming is essential, however, to keep these dogs looking their best, and stripping about twice a year on average will be required. In terms of temperament, West Highland Whites are typically lively, jaunty terriers. They prove alert guards at home, and need firm training from an early age, because, in spite of their small size, they can have rather dominant natures.

Westies enjoy a good run off the leash, especially if you have a ball for them to chase. It may be advisable to avoid areas where a number of other dogs are also being exercised, however, as these terriers are likely to prove rather possessive, and will not appreciate the involvement of others in their game.

YORKSHIRE TERRIER

ORIGINS *Yorkshire, England*	COAT TYPE/COLOUR *flowing; tan with* *dark bluish stripe*
HEIGHT *9 in (23 cm)*	WEIGHT *7 lb max (3.2 kg)*
CLASSIFICATION *toy/companion*	
NATURE *naturally friendly*	

2
SMALL BREEDS
DOGS BETWEEN 12 AND 18 in (30–45 cm)

A number of the larger members of the terrier group are featured here, along with dogs such as the Shar-pei and Basenji that are relatively new introductions on the international canine scene. The shorter hounds, such as the Beagle, are also included, as well as smaller spaniel breeds. When considering the size of dogs, it is worth remembering that the height of male dogs may be fractionally more than that of bitches. Where this affects the divisions in this book, the breed is grouped within the smaller size category.

AMERICAN COCKER SPANIEL

ORIGINS		COAT TYPE/COLOUR	
United States		*profuse; wide variety*	
HEIGHT		**WEIGHT**	
15 in (38 cm)		*24–28 lb (10.9–12.7 kg)*	
CLASSIFICATION			
gundog/sporting			
NATURE			
friendly; easy to train			

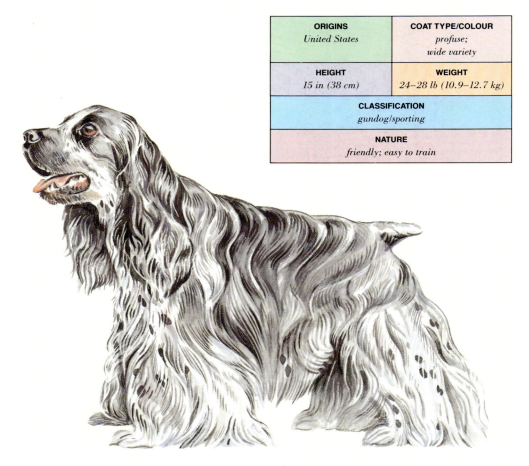

Originally bred from English Cocker Spaniels imported to the United States, this American form has been recognized as a separate breed since the 1940s. The American Cocker Spaniel was developed as a gundog, to take smaller game than its English counterpart, such as quail. Although shorter in stature, this should not be viewed principally as a pet dog. You will need to give these spaniels plenty of exercise.

The coat of the American Cocker is another distinguishing feature, being more profuse compared with the English form of the Cocker Spaniel. As a result, it needs extra care, and will benefit from a regular trim every two months or so. Regular inspection of the ears is also to be recommended, to minimize the risk of infections developing here. The upper part of the ear canal can be wiped over with damp cotton wool, but never be tempted to probe down into the canal itself. If your dog appears to be scratching at its ear repeatedly, your veterinarian will be able to inspect the canal and prescribe appropriate medication.

In terms of temperament, the American Cocker Spaniel usually proves easy to train and makes a good family pet. These spaniels are also available in a wide range of colours, ranging from solid colours such as black, chocolate or red, to tri-coloured and mixed parti-coloured forms. In the case of the solid colours, it is generally permitted to have a few white markings on the throat and chest, although, preferably, these should not be present. Certainly, small white areas elsewhere on the body will be penalized in the show ring.

BASENJI

ORIGINS	COAT TYPE/COLOUR
Zaire	*short; white, with red, black or black and tan*

HEIGHT	WEIGHT
17 in (43 cm)	*24 lb (10.9 kg)*

CLASSIFICATION	
hound/small hound	

NATURE	
very active, obedient, friendly	

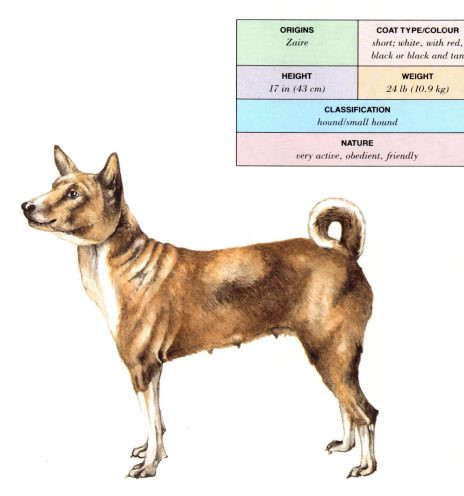

These unusual dogs originated in Zaïre, in Central Africa. Here they were kept by native tribes, remaining essentially unknown elsewhere until a pair were imported to Britain in 1936. These were exhibited at the famous Crufts Dog Show the following year, and caused a sensation. The breed was seen in the United States shortly afterwards, with the Basenji Club of America being formed here in 1942.

The Basenji is sometimes described as the Barkless Dog, but although it lacks the vocal range of other breeds, it is certainly not mute. It has a variety of calls, including a distinctive yodel, also described as a chortle. Basenjis should be offered green vegetables on a regular basis in addition to their normal diet, and will also eat grass. For this reason you must avoid using potentially harmful chemicals around the garden if you decide to keep this breed. They are very active dogs and need plenty of exercise, otherwise they will soon start to become obese.

In spite of coming from a tropical area, they are quite hardy. Their short coat, which can be red, black or black and tan, offset against white, is easy to keep in good condition with regular brushing. Alternatively, a hound glove can be used to give a good gloss to the coat. Basenjis will groom themselves rather like cats, licking their coats repeatedly.

Unfortunately, although Basenjis will live well alongside other pets, including cats and horses, they tend to disagree among themselves, and may have to be watched, at least until an order of dominance is established. Their breeding behaviour is different from that of other breeds, because bitches only come into season once rather than twice a year. This is usually between August and November, which means that puppies are only likely to be available in the spring.

BASSET HOUND

ORIGINS	COAT TYPE/COLOUR
France	*short; white with tan and black*
HEIGHT	**WEIGHT**
13–15 in (33–38 cm)	*40–51 lb (18.2–23.2 kg)*
CLASSIFICATION	
hound/small hound	
NATURE	
tenacious, greedy, friendly and tolerant	

This is another popular hound that is somewhat similar to the Basset, both in terms of appearance and temperament. It, too, is usually either lemon and white or a tri-coloured combination of black, white and tan, but its ears are much shorter than those of a Basset Hound. The origins of the Beagle are relatively obscure, although it is an old breed that has been kept for 500 years or so. These dogs were developed in Britain, and here, early in their history, wire-coated individuals were sometimes known, although today all Beagles are smooth-coated. There is still some variation in size, although the original small 'Pocket' Beagle, which faded out during the early years of the present century, is smaller than those seen today. It stood up to 10 in (25 cm) at the shoulder, whereas the smallest Beagles today are rarely less than 13 in (33 cm).

Beagles have proved highly adaptable by nature, and packs have been used to hunt a wide variety of game, ranging from rabbits in England to wild pigs in Sri Lanka. They may be accompanied on foot or horseback, and must have regular exercise if they are kept as pets. Persistent training is to be recommended from an early age, so as to ensure they will return when called, if they are running off the leash. Their short coats are easy to keep in top condition with very little grooming.

BEDLINGTON TERRIER

ORIGINS	COAT TYPE/COLOUR
Northumbria, England	*curly; blue/liver*
HEIGHT	**WEIGHT**
16 in (40.5 cm)	*18–23 lb (8.2–10.4 kg)*
CLASSIFICATION	
terrier	
NATURE	
active, playful; can be disagreeable with other dogs	

The term 'Basset' first appears in a book on hunting that was published in 1585 in France. Various different breeds of Basset were developed here, and the term itself appears to have come from the French word '*bas*', meaning 'low'. All Bassets are short-legged dogs, being bred initially from taller hounds. The Basset Hound itself is of relatively recent origin, derived from crosses involving the Basset Artesian Normand and the Bloodhound. It first achieved prominence in Britain at the end of the 1800s. Here the breed has been used to hunt rabbits, but in the United States it has been pitted against a wide range of game, including opossums.

As pack animals, Basset Hounds tend to be greedy by nature, and particular care needs to be taken with pet Bassets, to ensure that they do not become overweight, otherwise male dogs can suffer direct trauma to their penis from the ground. Regular daily walks are particularly vital with this breed. Typical Basset colours are lemon and white or a tri-coloured combination of black, white and tan.

Especially in the countryside, Basset Hounds will often set off in pursuit, regardless of their owner's instructions, if they pick up a scent. Like other hounds, they can be stubborn and relatively difficult to train, but Bassets are generally good-natured, and make lively companions, their loud, baritone bark carrying over a considerable distance. They do not suffer any inconvenience from their shortened legs, although it is probably best to choose the puppy with the straightest legs in the litter.

BEAGLE

ORIGINS	COAT TYPE/COLOUR
?Great Britain	*short; black, white and tan*
HEIGHT	**WEIGHT**
13–16 in (33–40.5 cm)	*18–30 lb (8.2–13.6 kg)*
CLASSIFICATION	
hound/small hound	
NATURE	
highly adaptable; persistent training required	

The rather manicured appearance of this breed belies a true terrier temperament. Its origins date back to the 1820s when Joseph Ainsley began the development of these terriers, naming them after the town in Northumbria, England, where he was living. Subsequent crosses involving Whippets gave the emerging breed a more streamlined appearance, with the sloping or 'roach' back still being evident in Bedlington Terriers today. The Dandie Dinmont Terrier was also used during its evolution, and is credited with contributing the characteristic top-knot of the breed.

The Bedlington has been used to hunt rats, its pace also proving useful against other animals, especially rabbits and hares. Their natural intelligence, coupled with a willingness to swim if necessary, meant that these terriers were popular companions for poachers. The tenacious nature of the Bedlington was also utilized in dog-fighting circles.

The coat of the Bedlington Terrier does not moult like that of most breeds, and so regular daily combing is needed to remove dead hairs. Trimming will also be necessary on occasion, to prevent the coat from becoming tangled while, for exhibition purposes, scissoring by hand is required, rather than stripping as with other terriers.

Bedlingtons are active dogs and quite playful, but they may not always agree with other dogs. They generally become a loyal, affectionate member of a family, however, and are quite patient with children, although this obviously depends to some extent on the individual dog. Bedlington Terriers are relatively easy to train.

BOSTON TERRIER

ORIGINS *United States*	COAT TYPE/COLOUR *short; white and black*
HEIGHT *15–17 in (38–43 cm)*	WEIGHT *15–20 lb (6.8–9 kg)*
CLASSIFICATION *utility/non-sporting/companion*	
NATURE *good companion*	

The Bulldog has undergone a dramatic change in appearance during its long history, particularly since the development of show standards over the past century. In their early years, Bulldogs were used for bull-baiting, and tended to be a longer-legged breed than those seen today. After bull-baiting was banned in 1835 in Britain, it was also involved in dog-fighting, but Bulldogs proved less popular for this purpose than the Bull Terrier. The breed could then have slipped into obscurity but was rescued to become a popular show dog.

Today, the Bulldog has evolved into a placid and phlegmatic dog with a somewhat comical appearance. However, it is a solid, muscular animal with powerful jaws. Criticisms of the breed have been made because of its respiratory and reproductive problems, with Caesarean section births being common because of its relatively large head.

Bulldogs suffer badly from heat stress and should not be exercised during the warmest part of the day. In addition, they must never be kept enclosed in a car on their own in the summer. *All* dogs are vulnerable to heat stress in such surroundings, but Bulldogs in particular are liable to die very rapidly under these conditions. They tend not to want a lot of exercise, but should be given a daily walk, as this will help to prevent them from becoming obese.

CAVALIER KING CHARLES SPANIEL

ORIGINS *United States*	COAT TYPE/COLOUR *silky; tan and white*
HEIGHT *12–13 in (30.5–33 cm)*	WEIGHT *12–18 lb (5.4–8.2 kg)*
CLASSIFICATION *terrier/companion*	
NATURE *highly affectionate, sometimes nervous*	

This American breed was developed during the latter part of the last century, with various strains of Bulldog, Bull Terrier and Boxer all contributing to its ancestry. Indeed, these dogs were originally called American Bull Terriers for a period, until objection from Bull Terrier owners forced a change of name. The breed was finally recognized in 1893 by the American Kennel Club as the Boston Terrier.

Since then, it has become widely known throughout the world. They have proved easy dogs to train and make delightful companions. Boston Terriers are quite at home even in urban surroundings, and will walk happily on a leash if it is not possible to give them a daily run. Nevertheless, they do enjoy a period of freedom, to explore in the company of their owner.

The short coat of this breed is easy to groom and is never shed profusely, which makes housework easier. Boston Terriers may snuffle because of their compact noses, while their relatively prominent eyes are prone to injury, especially if they charge off through undergrowth. However, the most significant problem associated with these terriers is only apparent during the whelping period. The relatively large head, coupled with a narrow pelvis, often causes problems when a bitch is giving birth. A Caesarean section may be required if a puppy's head becomes stuck in the birth canal. Particular care is therefore necessary when breeding Boston Terriers.

BULLDOG

ORIGINS		COAT TYPE/COLOUR
Britain		*short;*
		tan
HEIGHT		**WEIGHT**
12–14 in (30.5–35.5 cm)		*55 lb (25 kg)*
CLASSIFICATION		
utility/non-sporting/guard		
NATURE		
placid and phlegmatic		

This breed is a re-creation of the type of spaniel that can be seen in old paintings. Its development came about as a result of a quest by Roswell Eldridge, an American who offered large cash prizes at Crufts Dog Show during the 1920s to attract breeders with this type of dog. The Cavalier can now be distinguished from the ordinary King Charles Spaniel by the flattened, rather than domed, appearance of its skull between the eyes, and its longer, less compact nose. It has developed into a slightly larger dog.

In terms of temperament, however, these two breeds are very similar, and they are bred in the same colours. In both cases, the coats of puppies are far less profuse than those of adults, which need regular brushing to maintain their attractive silky appearance. They make good companion dogs for people of all ages and are highly affectionate by nature.

CHOW CHOW

ORIGINS	COAT TYPE/COLOUR
China	*profuse;* *bronze*
HEIGHT	**WEIGHT**
18 in min (45.5 cm)	*55–60 lb (25–27.2 kg)*
CLASSIFICATION	
utility/non-sporting/companion	
NATURE	
often loyal, sometimes bad-tempered	

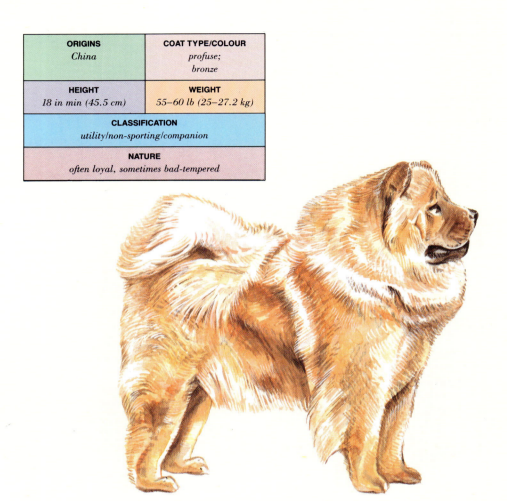

This ancient Chinese breed has served a variety of purposes since its development many thousands of years ago. Its history is said to date back to the eleventh century BC, and in these early years Chow Chows were kept for hunting purposes. One Chinese emperor is said to have maintained a kennel of 5,000 of these dogs, cared for by 10,000 people! Subsequently, the breed was kept as a source of food, with young dogs being reared solely for this purpose on a diet comprised mainly of grain. The Chow Chow has also been used as a means of transporting goods and pulling sledges, and its fur has been made into clothing.

Chow Chows were first seen in Britain during the latter part of the eighteenth century, and were originally exhibited as wild dogs. They later gained more widespread acceptability when kept by Queen Victoria. Unfortunately, in spite of their close association with people, Chow Chows are not always the best-tempered of dogs. They can also be very difficult to train, compared with other breeds. Yet the Chow Chow often develops into a loyal companion, preferring to live with an individual person rather than as a family dog.

A good brushing is required to keep its coat in good condition, especially in the case of a long-coated dog. Regular exercise, preferably away from other dogs, is essential as well. As show dogs, Chow Chows often reign supreme, and a member of this breed holds the record out of all breeds for the greatest number of Challenge Certificates ever won.

CLUMBER SPANIEL

ORIGINS	COAT TYPE/COLOUR
?France	*smooth; lemon (or orange) and white*
HEIGHT	**WEIGHT**
16–18 in (40.5–45.5 cm)	*55–70 lb (25–31.8 kg)*
CLASSIFICATION	
gundog/sporting	
NATURE	
good sporting companion; sturdy	

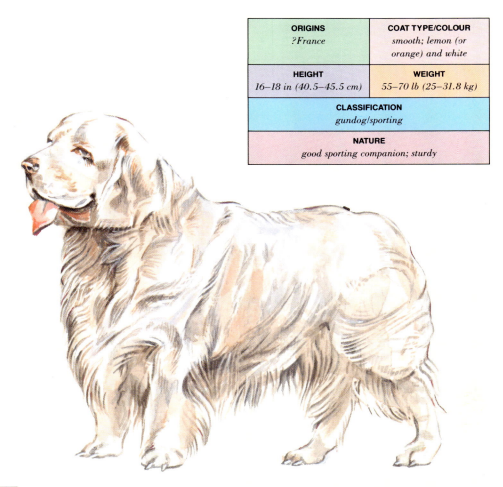

The stocky Clumber is the heaviest of all the spaniels, with dogs of this breed weighing up to 70 lb (32 kg). Its precise origins are unclear, but it is probably descended from French stock obtained by the Duke of Newcastle over a century ago. The breed was actually named after the Duke's estate, Clumber Park.

Although not ranking as one of the most common spaniels, the Clumber is still highly valued as a sporting companion. It was developed for its scenting skills, but also proves versatile enough to make a good retriever as well. Clumber Spaniels may not be as agile as some breeds, but there is no doubting their stamina. This is not a suitable companion in an urban environment, however, preferring more spacious surroundings where it can have plenty of exercise.

The coat of this breed is somewhat less profuse than in other spaniels and mud will brush out easily once it has dried. In terms of coloration, Clumber Spaniels are invariably lemon and white or orange and white, with paler markings generally being preferred. Their feet are covered with dense hair, and, especially after exercise in the summer months, you must check for grass seeds that may have become tangled up here. These could otherwise penetrate into the feet and track up the leg, causing a painful injury.

COCKER SPANIEL
(ENGLISH COCKER SPANIEL)

ORIGINS	COAT TYPE/COLOUR
Wales; south-west England	*silky; wide variety*
HEIGHT	**WEIGHT**
16–18 in (40.5–45.5 cm)	*55–70 lb (25–31.8 kg)*
CLASSIFICATION	
gundog/sporting	
NATURE	
sociable, sometimes aggressive	

Acknowledged as the national dog of Finland, the Finnish Spitz shows the unmistakable characteristics of this northern group of dogs. Its alert demeanour, with pricked ears and the curly tail that extends forward over the back, reflects a breed that has evolved to flush game birds such as the capercaillie from cover for waiting guns. Its tracking skills have also been used to pursue bear and elk. The appearance of the Finnish Spitz, in terms of an official standard, was first established back in 1812.

Only quite recently, however, has it become popular elsewhere. In Britain, Lady Kitty Ritson did much to draw attention to the breed during the 1920s and 1930s. The Finnish Spitz is a hardy, yet home-loving breed, with plenty of stamina. It will thrive in a family environment and also makes an alert guard dog in these surroundings. However, a possible drawback associated with the breed can be its tendency to bark repeatedly. This behaviour is related to its hunting technique, the dog having been encouraged to bark to indicate the presence of a bird in a tree. This breed is still judged on its barking abilities in working trials held in its country of origin.

FOX TERRIERS:
WIRE AND SMOOTH

ORIGINS	COAT TYPE/COLOUR
Great Britain	*smooth/wiry; black, white and tan*
HEIGHT	**WEIGHT**
16 in (40.5 cm)	*16–18 lb (7.3–8.2 kg)*
CLASSIFICATION	
terrier	
NATURE	
inquisitive and lively	

Officially, in Britain, the Kennel Club recognizes this breed just as the Cocker Spaniel, but as American breeders sometimes refer to their breed under the same name, this designation has been made to avoid possible confusion. The description of 'cocker' probably originated from the use of these dogs in the hunting of woodcock, which were considered something of a delicacy. Regional differences played a part in the development of the spaniel breeds in Britain, with the Cocker itself evolving in parts of Wales and south-west England.

In spite of their popularity as pets, Cocker Spaniels still retain a strong desire to work and today they are often used to scent and flush rabbits. They can also be taught to retrieve game after it has been shot. Cocker Spaniels enjoy human company and are generally keen to please, so training presents no particular problems. However, there has been a tendency for some unpleasant behavioural characteristics to develop within certain bloodlines, which can be reflected in unexpected aggressive outbursts. Responsible breeders have sought to eliminate this problem, but puppies of unknown origin may present more of a risk in this respect. English Cockers are available in a wide range of colours, like their American counterpart.

FINNISH SPITZ

ORIGINS	COAT TYPE/COLOUR
Finland	*shaggy; reddish*
HEIGHT	**WEIGHT**
17–20 in (43–51 cm)	*31–36 lb (14–16.3 kg)*
CLASSIFICATION	
hound/small hound	
NATURE	
hardy and home-loving	

Both the Wire- and Smooth-coated Fox Terriers share a common ancestry and are thought to be the descendants of some of the old terrier breeds of England, crossed with hounds. They were used for hunting purposes, and have remained active dogs best suited to a country environment today.

In an earlier stage in their history, it was usual to cross both coat types together, but they are now recognized as separate breeds. Undoubtedly, the Smooth Fox Terrier is the easier form to care for, its short coat needing just an occasional brushing to remain in good condition. The Wire Fox Terrier will need stripping, to remove dead hairs from the coat.

This can be carried out by hand, but will prove to be a time-consuming process, so pet owners may resort to having their dogs trimmed instead. Nevertheless, the Wire Fox Terrier has become a very popular breed internationally, a well-manicured show dog looking both impressive and appealing. In terms of temperament, these are typical terriers, with inquisitive and lively natures.

GLEN OF IMAAL TERRIER

ORIGINS	COAT TYPE/COLOUR
Ireland	*rough;* *brindle blue/wheaten*
HEIGHT	**WEIGHT**
14 in (35.5 cm)	*30–35 lb (13.6–15.9 kg)*
NATURE	
courageous and playful	

Aminiature form of the Greyhound is known to have existed over 2,000 years ago. Subsequently, such dogs became especially fashionable during the sixteenth century in Italy. Here they were kept simply as pets by members of the Italian nobility and soon these miniature Greyhounds were in demand across Europe. Although the trend towards the breeding of an even smaller version caused serious problems for the breed in the second half of the nineteenth century, today the Italian Greyhound is again as sturdy as ever, averaging about 14 in (36 cm) in height and weighing approximately 8 lb (3.6 kg).

Italian Greyhounds are quiet and responsive dogs, with affectionate natures. They will enjoy a brisk run off the leash every day, but if the weather is inclement, they should be protected by a coat, as these dogs are sensitive to the cold and may develop kidney problems if chilled. In spite of their speed, they can be trained to return quite easily, and make an ideal companion for young or old alike. Much of the stock available in Europe today actually has a North American ancestry, as many dogs were imported from the United States after the Second World War, to ensure that European bloodlines were preserved.

JACK RUSSELL TERRIER

ORIGINS	COAT TYPE/COLOUR
Devon, England	*short;* *white, black and tan*
HEIGHT	**WEIGHT**
10–15 in (25–38 cm)	*10 lb + (4.5 kg)*
NATURE	
lively, excitable	

One of the more unusual terrier breeds that is now attracting increasing interest, the Glen of Imaal Terrier is actually an old breed, developed in the vicinity of County Wicklow, Ireland. Here it was used to hunt badgers and, for a period, as a fighting dog. This rather anti-social side to the Glen of Imaal Terrier is still apparent to some extent today; although they agree well with people, these terriers do not relish the company of other dogs.

The Glen of Imaal Terrier is a tough and hardy breed, with a brave nature. It also has a playful side to its character, and enjoys a good chase after a ball. These terriers are best kept in fairly rural surroundings, but will adapt to urban life provided that they can be exercised away from other dogs. Glen of Imaal Terriers are bred in either brindle, blue or wheaten colours, and their harsh coats need a thorough brushing each day. Although, at the present time, the breed is not recognized by the American Kennel Club, many American fanciers, as elsewhere, are falling under the charm of these courageous terriers.

ITALIAN GREYHOUND

ORIGINS	COAT TYPE/COLOUR
Italy	*very fine, soft; liver and white*
HEIGHT	**WEIGHT**
13–15 in (33–38 cm)	*6–10 lb (2.7-4.5 kg)*
CLASSIFICATION	
toy/coursing	
NATURE	
quiet, responsive; sensitive to cold	

One of the most widely recognized terriers, the Jack Russell has a long ancestry, dating back over a century. It is named after the Revd Jack Russell, who was popularly described as the 'Hunting Parson' because of his keen interest in fox hunting. Russell lived in Devon, England, and here, during the latter part of the last century, he began to create a strain of versatile hunting terriers. He wanted dogs that would be able to hunt alongside hounds, and were also capable of going to earth and driving out a fox.

An influential member of the Kennel Club during its formative years, the Revd Russell nevertheless vehemently opposed the creation of an official standard for this breed. He feared that this would actually weaken its character.

As a result, the Jack Russell has remained a breed in everything but name. Moves are now afoot to change this situation in various countries, however, and widespread formal recognition is likely to take place before long.

In terms of temperament, the Jack Russell is a lively and rather excitable dog. It can sometimes prove snappy, but this is the exception rather than the rule. In addition to its original hunting skills, the Jack Russell has proved to be a dedicated ratter, although it does not appear that its creator used these dogs for this task. As a result, they can be particularly vulnerable to leptospirosis as this infection is often spread by rats. As with all dogs, Jack Russells should be routinely vaccinated against this serious bacterial disease.

KEESHOND

ORIGINS	COAT TYPE/COLOUR
Netherlands	*fluffy; wolf-grey*
HEIGHT	**WEIGHT**
18 in (45.5 cm)	*55–66 lb (25–30 kg)*
CLASSIFICATION	
utility/non-sporting/companion	
NATURE	
alert, intelligent, playful	

Another of the ancient Tibetan breeds, the Lhasa Apso used to be given as a gift to the Chinese court by the Dalai Lama who ruled Tibet. The unusual name of these dogs translates as 'goat-like', and it may have been that their ancestors were actually kept as guardians for herds of goats before they acquired regal status. Traditionally, they lived inside homes, with the Tibetan Mastiff being kept as a guard outside. Lhasa Apsos first reached the West in the early years of the present century, and there was initially some confusion between these dogs and the larger Tibetan Terrier. By the 1930s, however, the Lhasa was established in its own right, and has since become the most commonly seen of the four Tibetan breeds.

They are attractive, affectionate dogs, but their long, flowing coats obviously need careful grooming on a daily basis, otherwise the hair will become badly tangled and, in extreme cases, the dog may have to be anaesthetized to have the mats removed painlessly. As companions, there are few dogs as long-lived, with Lhasa Apsos frequently living into their late teens and beyond – up to 29 years in one astonishing case!

POODLES: MINIATURE AND STANDARD

ORIGINS	COAT TYPE/COLOUR
?Britain	*shaggy, curly; wide variety*
HEIGHT	**WEIGHT**
11–15 in (28–38 cm); 15 in + (38 cm)	*26 lb (11.8 kg); 49 lb (22.2 kg)*
CLASSIFICATION	
utility/non-sporting/companion	
NATURE	
intelligent, friendly companion	

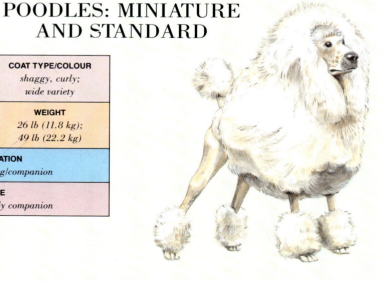

Descended from spitz stock, the ancestors of this breed were a common sight on barges travelling along the River Rhine. They are believed to be named after two leaders of the Dutch Patriot Party, who adopted the breed as a symbol during the eighteenth century. Both these men had the Christian name of Kees, but this link ultimately had an adverse effect on the popularity of the Keeshond (pronounced 'Kayshond') when the Prince of Orange took power in the Netherlands.

During the present century, however, Keeshonden (the plural form) have attracted increasing attention from dog-lovers, with a member of this breed winning the top award at Crufts in 1957. They are wolf-grey in colour, with an attractive fluffy coat. The ruff around the neck is more prominent in adult dogs than puppies. Avoid using a check chain of any kind when training a Keeshond, as this may damage its ruff. A thorough daily grooming will be necessary to keep the coat in top condition, while proper training is required because these dogs can prove to be independent and strong-willed. Keeshonden are quite at home in the domestic environment, and can be relied upon as keen guards. Their bell-like bark is characteristic of the breed.

LHASA APSO

ORIGINS	COAT TYPE/COLOUR
Tibet	*long, flowing; smoky-grey, white, brown*

HEIGHT	WEIGHT
10 in (25 cm)	*13–15 lb (5.9–6.8 kg)*

CLASSIFICATION	
utility/non-sporting/companion	

NATURE	
alert, intelligent; long-lived	

The Standard form of the Poodle, measuring over 15 in (38 cm) at the shoulder, is believed to be the oldest of the three breeds. It is a lively and intelligent dog, which first became known in Britain during the seventeenth century. Standards can be obtained in all the usual Poodle colours, which vary from white through cream and apricot to brown, blue and black. Only solid colours are acceptable, but the depth of coloration of puppies is likely to vary until the dog is perhaps 18 months old.

Although the popularity of the Standard Poodle has waned during recent years, the Miniature form, averaging between 11–15 in (28–38 cm) in height, has grown in popularity. It is a smaller breed but otherwise identical in appearance, and can be kept in more compact surroundings.

In common with other Poodles, the Miniature may suffer more from dental problems than other breeds. You should therefore routinely inspect the mouths of these dogs, brushing their teeth regularly with a special canine toothpaste. If deposits of tartar do accumulate on the teeth, especially close to the gums, then arrange with your veterinarian to have this removed by descaling as soon as possible. Otherwise, the bacteria in this plaque are likely to damage the teeth and can also cause gum disease.

PULI

ORIGINS	COAT TYPE/COLOUR
Hungary	*dreadlocked; black/grey*
HEIGHT	**WEIGHT**
16–17½ in (40.5–45.5 cm)	*28½–33 lb (12.9–15 kg)*
CLASSIFICATION	
working/hound	
NATURE	
loyal, intelligent	

It appears that this breed has existed in Belgium for well over 300 years, although its precise ancestry is unknown. It has been suggested that it could be a miniature form of a black Belgian Shepherd Dog, or, alternatively, could have a spitz ancestry. The Schipperke was certainly very popular among shoemakers in Belgium during the seventeenth century. Such dogs were paraded wearing ornate collars made of brass, and possibly took part in the earliest specialist dog show ever held, when a Schipperke show was organized by the Belgian Guild of Workmen in 1690.

Their unusual name actually translates from the Flemish as 'little captain'. The breed was a popular choice among barge-owners, alerting them to the presence of strangers who might want to come aboard. The interest expressed by the Queen of Belgium in 1885 helped the breed to become popular as a fashionable pet. Schipperkes are usually black in colour, and their coat is easy to keep in top condition. These are hardy and affectionate dogs and make good family pets. They will benefit from a good daily walk, but prove to be quite happy in an urban environment.

SCHNAUZER: MINIATURE AND STANDARD

ORIGINS	COAT TYPE/COLOUR
Germany	*long; grey and white*
HEIGHT	**WEIGHT**
14 in (35.5 cm); 19 in (48 cm)	*13–15 lb (5.9–6.8 kg); 33 lb (15 kg)*
CLASSIFICATION	
utility/toy/companion; utility/working/gundog	
NATURE	
lively, playful; wary of strangers	

Although it may appear that a Puli's coat is somehow prepared by artificial means, its dreadlocks are actually quite natural. The breed originated in Hungary, and its name is derived from the words *puli hou*. This translates literally as 'destroyer Huns', and refers to a tribe of Magyar warriors who invaded Hungary from the East about 1,000 years ago, bringing with them their livestock, which included the ancestors of the Puli. The plural form of their name is *Pulix* in Hungary, but tends to be *Pulik* elsewhere. These are herding dogs, originally used to watch over flocks of sheep.

The traditional form of the Puli appears to be black, but grey forms are also known. In spite of its rather unkempt appearance, the Puli's coat needs considerable attention. The individual cords, which tend to be thinner in dogs kept in North America and Europe than in Hungary itself, must be carefully groomed by hand. Proper brushing will also be necessary to maintain their distinctive appearance.

The Puli only became known outside Hungary at the end of the Second World War. Occasionally, in the United States, you may see their coats prepared in a woolly 'Afro' style, although the corded appearance is still more typical. They have proved to be both loyal and intelligent companions, as reflected in their working ancestry.

SCHIPPERKE

ORIGINS		COAT TYPE/COLOUR	
?Belgium		*shaggy; usually black*	
HEIGHT		WEIGHT	
10–13 in (25–33 cm)		*12–16 lb (5.4–7.3 kg)*	
CLASSIFICATION			
utility/non-sporting/companion			
NATURE			
hardy and affectionate			

Three different types of Schnauzer have been developed and all share a common ancestry. The Giant Schnauzer measures about 25 in (63.5 cm) at the shoulder, but these two forms are much smaller, standing approximately 14 in (35.5 cm) and 19 in (48 cm) tall, respectively. They are of German origin, with the word *Schnauze* translating as 'muzzle', and describing the characteristic longer hair here, which is a feature of these breeds.

The Standard Schnauzer existed as long ago as the seventeenth century, being used as a cattle dog and also valued for its rat-catching abilities. It first became known in show circles in the late 1800s, as the Wire-haired Pinscher, before being recognized under its present name. Selection of the smallest dogs from litters of the Standard Schnauzer, and resulting crossings of these, probably with the Affenpinscher, eventually led to the development of the Miniature Schnauzer.

Their wiry coat needs a good daily brushing, and you may also have to wash the hair around the mouth if it becomes soiled with food. The use of a dried or semi-moist dog food can be useful in preventing this problem. A regular trim every few months is required to keep the coat immaculate. This can be carried out at your local grooming parlour.

Schnauzers of all sizes will prove lively dogs, who enjoy a good game. They are very devoted to members of the family, but are rather suspicious of strangers. As guard dogs, they will give an early indication of intruders.

SHAR-PEI

ORIGINS	COAT TYPE/COLOUR
China	*short; wide variety*
HEIGHT	**WEIGHT**
18–20 in (45.5–51 cm)	*44–55 lb (20–25 kg)*
NATURE	
exuberant and loving	

Affectionately known as the Sheltie, this breed is said to have evolved on the Shetland Islands, off the north coast of Scotland. Here they were kept by the crofters who scratched a living from this rather inhospitable terrain. The Shetland Sheepdog probably developed from a range of dogs brought to these islands over the years, but has been established as a pure breed for over a century. It is very similar to the Rough Collie, although smaller in size.

Shelties are intelligent and easily trained, often featuring in obedience competitions. They have been developed in a wide range of colours, with tri-colours being among the most striking.

In such cases, the deep tan creates an attractive contrast against their black and white markings. The blue merle is an unusual shade of clear silvery blue, mixed with black and often with tan coloration as well.

The coat of the Sheltie is relatively soft and light and a firm brushing each day should keep it free from tangles. In terms of exercise, Shelties are quite active dogs and need sufficient space for a good run. They are generally quite trustworthy with other dogs, however, and therefore can be allowed off the leash in a suitable area in a park without fear of them provoking any disturbance.

STAFFORDSHIRE BULL TERRIER

ORIGINS	COAT TYPE/COLOUR
England	*short; wide variety*
HEIGHT	**WEIGHT**
14–16 in (35.5–40.5 cm)	*28–38 lb (12.7–17.3 kg)*
CLASSIFICATION	
terrier	
NATURE	
loyal; can be aggressive	

Having been in danger of extinction during the late 1960s. this ancient Chinese breed has since attracted the attention of dog fanciers throughout the world, and its future is now assured. Its origins date back over 2,000 years, and it may have a common ancestry with the Chow Chow, with which it shares the unique characteristic of having a blue tongue. A recent addition to the British show scene, at one stage Shar-peis were kept as fighting dogs, their loose folds of skin enabling them to wriggle free from an opponent and strike back. These days are thankfully long past, and, in terms of temperament, the contemporary Shar-pei is an exuberant and loving companion.

The rescue of the breed was achieved through the efforts of a Hong Kong breeder called Matgo Law. Directly as a result of his appeal in the dog press, American enthusiasts imported Shar-peis and the breed was then taken to Britain and other European countries. Although the first litter of Shar-peis was only produced in 1982 in Britain, the breed has since become a relatively common sight. There can be a problem associated with it, however, which breeders are now trying to eliminate. Bacterial infections may develop in skin folds if these are excessive, and Shar-peis are also prone to an abnormality affecting the eyelids, called entropion. This is likely to need surgical correction before the eyelashes can damage the cornea and affect the dog's sight.

SHETLAND SHEEPDOG

ORIGINS	COAT TYPE/COLOUR
Shetland Islands	*soft and light; wide variety*
HEIGHT	**WEIGHT**
14½ in (37 cm)	*14–16 lb (6.4–7.3 kg)*
CLASSIFICATION	
working/hound	
NATURE	
active; trustworthy with other dogs	

Crossings of terriers with Bulldogs during the early years of the nineteenth century gave rise to the origins of this breed. It was developed for dog-fighting purposes in England, but when this activity was made illegal, breeders sought to remove aggressive traits from its nature. Recognition was slow in coming, however, the Kennel Club of Great Britain only acknowledging the Staffordshire Bull Terrier in 1935.

These are relatively stubborn dogs by nature, and still retain a tendency to scrap with other dogs that cross their path. Firm training is therefore essential from the outset, especially if you keep one of these terriers in an urban area, where it is more likely to come into contact with other dogs. They tend to make loyal house pets, however, and prove determined guards of property.

The Staffordshire Bull Terrier was recognized by the American Kennel Club in 1974. A slightly different form is also popular here, classified separately as the American Staffordshire Terrier, often abbreviated to AmStaffs. These are not the same as the fearsome American Pit Bull Terrier, but resemble their English ancestor in temperament. A good choice of colour is available in the case of both Staffordshire breeds.

SUSSEX SPANIEL

ORIGINS	COAT TYPE/COLOUR
Sussex, England	*silky; golden liver*
HEIGHT	**WEIGHT**
15–16 in (38–40.5 cm)	*45 lb (20.4 kg)*
CLASSIFICATION	
gundog/sporting	
NATURE	
placid; hard-working	

In spite of its name, this breed is not derived from terrier stock, but was originally bred in Tibet as a herding dog. There was some confusion among the various Tibetan breeds when they first became more widely known in the West during the early years of the present century, but the Tibetan Terrier was subsequently acknowledged by the Kennel Club in Great Britain during 1937. In the United States, it was only recognized for showing purposes as recently as 1973.

Aside from their herding activities, these shaggy dogs were highly valued as companions in their homeland, and the reasons for this are not hard to recognize today. They are happy, friendly dogs with a tolerant disposition towards children. Their coat, which is now more profuse than in the past, creating a very elegant appearance, will need daily brushing to prevent it from becoming tangled.

These terriers can be bred in a wide range of colours, with only liver or chocolate being frowned upon in show circles. While in its early days the Tibetan Terrier was shown in a tousled state, many hours of preparatory work are now essential when benching these dogs.

WHIPPET

ORIGINS	COAT TYPE/COLOUR
northern England	*short; wide variety*
HEIGHT	**WEIGHT**
18½ in (47 cm)	*18–28 lb (8.2–12.7 kg)*
CLASSIFICATION	
hound/coursing	
NATURE	
quiet, responsive; sensitive to cold	

This breed of spaniel was developed in the English county of Sussex during the 1790s. Sussex Spaniels have never been especially common, but their placid and hard-working nature made them highly valued both as gun-dogs and companions. The breed nearly vanished into obscurity towards the end of the last century, and it was only in the 1950s that its future became more secure. During recent years, for whatever reason, it has undergone something of a revival.

The Sussex Spaniel is a distinctive shade of golden-liver, with this coloration being broken only by a white chest spot in some individuals. This is considered a show fault, in contrast to the situation in a number of other breeds of spaniel. It has never established a following as a pet dog, as it strongly retains its tough working instincts. For this reason, the Sussex Spaniel is most suited to a rural environment and requires considerable exercise by way of daily walks.

TIBETAN TERRIER

ORIGINS		COAT TYPE/COLOUR
Tibet		*shaggy;* *wide variety*
HEIGHT		**WEIGHT**
14–16 in (35.5–40.5 cm)		*18–30 lb (8.2–13.6 kg)*
CLASSIFICATION		
utility/non-sporting/companion		
NATURE		
very hardy, affectionate		

Developed for its speed in the north of England, the Whippet used to be known as the poor man's racehorse. These dogs were raced over straight tracks, which were typically 200 yd (183 m) long, being thrown into the course by their owners. The fastest individuals could reach the finish within 11½ seconds, and even today the Greyhound is not a match for a Whippet in terms of pace over such distances.

A combination of small Greyhounds and terriers contributed to its ancestry, with a later contribution from the Italian Greyhound. The breed was introduced to the United States by emigrants from England during the early years of the present century. Although no longer kept primarily for their pace, Whippets have now found a new following in show circles and as a household pet. They are very trustworthy with children, but can sometimes prove nervous in unfamiliar surroundings.

No restriction is imposed on their coloration by either the Kennel Club or the American Kennel Club (which did not recognize the breed until 1976), and as grooming of their short coats is straightforward, this breed makes an ideal introduction to the show ring. Whippets are adaptable dogs. Although they may chase hares in the country, they will settle well in the town, provided they can have a short, brisk run off the leash every day. In cold or wet weather, they should be fitted with a coat to protect them against the elements when they are out of doors, as they are not a particularly hardy breed.

3
MEDIUM-SIZED BREEDS

DOGS BETWEEN 18 AND 24 in (45–60 cm)

Within this grouping can be found the popular retrievers and the various collies. The largest of the terrier breeds and some relative newcomers such as the Vizsla also fall into this category. It needs to be remembered, however, that the larger the dog, the greater will be the cost of keeping it. This is a direct reflection of their food requirements. The labelling on dog foods generally lists the suggested amounts needed by different breeds. As a rough guide, the dogs featured in this section will need between one and a half and two and a half 14 oz (400 g) cans daily, with a corresponding volume of biscuit meal, typically given in two feeds: in the morning and early evening.

AIREDALE TERRIER

ORIGINS	COAT TYPE/COLOUR
Yorkshire, England	*smooth; black and tan*

HEIGHT	WEIGHT
23–24 in (58.5–61 cm)	*44 lb (20 kg)*

CLASSIFICATION
terrier

NATURE
intelligent, alert and tough

The largest of the terrier breeds, the Airedale is named after the River Aire in Yorkshire, England, where it was first bred. Here it was originally known by a variety of local names, such as the Bingley and the Waterside Terrier. Its present name was established at the Airedale Agricultural Show in 1879.

Airedale Terriers are thought to be descended from the now extinct Black and Tan Terrier, with crossings involving Otterhounds also playing a part in its ancestry. The Airedale has been used for hunting a variety of game, ranging from rats to foxes and badgers. Its intelligent and alert nature has led to its involvement in police work, and the breed was a popular choice as a messenger dog, working in the trenches during the First World War.

Today, these terriers are a frequent sight at dog shows around the world, although for show purposes their coat has to be stripped by hand, which is an onerous task. Airedales are tough dogs and may occasionally become embroiled in a fight with another dog, but they are not aggressive by nature. They will prove formidable guards, however, being very loyal to their owner. In terms of exercise, they do need a good run every day, otherwise they may become bored and destructive.

BEARDED COLLIE

ORIGINS	COAT TYPE/COLOUR
the border counties, *Great Britain*	*flowing*

HEIGHT	WEIGHT
21–22 in (53.5–56 cm)	*66 lb (30 kg)*

CLASSIFICATION	
working/herding	

NATURE	
lovable, playful	

An old breed, the Bearded Collie appears to have originated in the border area between Scotland and England; dogs of similar appearance have been known here since the eighteenth century. They were originally working dogs, kept for herding sheep and cattle. Their origins may be traced back to the Polish Lowland Sheepdog, which was said to have been brought to Scotland as long ago as 1514 by sailors who swapped these dogs for sheep.

By the 1930s, however, the Bearded Collie had declined dramatically in numbers, almost to the point of extinction. It was saved largely through the efforts of Mrs Willison, whose Bothkennar 'Beardies' formed the basis of all today's bloodlines. The breed has since gained in popularity and took the Best in Show award at Crufts in 1989. These are lovable, playful dogs, but you must be prepared to give them adequate exercise, which includes a good daily run, and spend plenty of time grooming their long and flowing coats. In addition, they have become a popular breed in the United States during recent years.

BORDER COLLIE

ORIGINS	COAT TYPE/COLOUR
the border counties, Great Britain	*smooth; black and white*
HEIGHT	**WEIGHT**
21 in (53.5 cm)	*40–50lb (18.2–22.7 kg)*
NATURE	
very receptive to training; good family dog	

The history of the Boxer dates back to the 1830s. Among the breeds that contributed to its ancestry, it is thought that the Bulldog was responsible for introducing the white coloration evident in Boxers today. Great Danes and French Bulldogs may also have been used in the Boxer's development. This breed did not immediately gain a strong following outside its native Germany, and only began to attract attention elsewhere after the First World War.

Few dogs are more playful by nature than Boxers and they are ideal for a home with bigger children, although they are perhaps rather too boisterous to live alongside toddlers. As may be imagined, Boxers need adequate space for their active natures. They are highly affectionate and loyal companions, and can be trained quite easily. Indeed, they have been used as police dogs in various countries. Their short coats require little attention.

Sadly, Boxers are often quite short-lived, being highly susceptible to a wide range of tumours. Ten years is often the upper limit, although, as veterinary medicine has advanced, it has proved possible to combat some tumours quite effectively.

BRITTANY SPANIEL
(BRITTANY)

ORIGINS	COAT TYPE/COLOUR
France	*silky; wide variety*
HEIGHT	**WEIGHT**
17½–20½ in (44.5–52 cm)	*30–40 lb (13.6–18.2 kg)*
CLASSIFICATION	
gundog/sporting	
NATURE	
sensitive; easy to train	

A true working dog, the Border Collie is another of the breeds that originated in the border counties. It is usually black and white in colour, with some individuals having longer coats than others. There has been less standardization within this breed than many others; in fact, a standard was only drawn up for the Border Collie by the Kennel Club in 1976. It is always a popular competitor at obedience competitions, and a frequent winner.

Nevertheless, although these collies are among the most receptive of all breeds to training, they really do not settle well in a purely domestic environment. Here they will become bored and frequently turn destructive as a result. As companion dogs in a rural area, however, where they can work and use their natural intelligence, Border Collies will be a source of great pleasure, as well as proving protective towards all members of the family.

BOXER

ORIGINS	COAT TYPE/COLOUR
Germany	*short; white and tan*
HEIGHT	**WEIGHT**
22–24 in (58.5–61 cm)	*66 lb (30 kg)*
CLASSIFICATION	
working/guard dog	
NATURE	
boisterous, highly affectionate; short life-span	

This French breed was effectively re-created at the turn of the present century, having been on the verge of extinction. It is more reminiscent of a setter than a spaniel, both in terms of its appearance and its behaviour. As a consequence, the American Kennel Club has recently changed its name simply to the Brittany. As a working dog – commonly seen at field trials rather than shows – it has proved a talented pointer and has a keen scenting nose.

The Brittany Spaniel has a sensitive nature and is correspondingly easy to train, being very responsive to its owner's wishes. In terms of coloration, these dogs can be either orange, maroon or black combined with white, while tri-coloured forms are also recognized. You must be prepared to give the Brittany plenty of exercise; although it does make a good pet, it is still a working dog as well and this should be reflected in its surroundings.

BULL TERRIER

ORIGINS	COAT TYPE/COLOUR
England	*short; wide variety*
HEIGHT	**WEIGHT**
21–22 in (53.5–56 cm)	*52–62 lb (23.6–28.1 kg)*
CLASSIFICATION	
terrier	
NATURE	
determined, powerful, but normally trustworthy	

Collies were another of the herding dogs originally bred in Scotland, although their ancestors may have come from Iceland. They first attracted widespread attention when Queen Victoria brought some of these dogs back to her kennels after a visit to Scotland in 1860. The Rough Collie has since become by far the most popular of the two forms, helped perhaps by its involvement in the various *Lassie* films.

Both the Smooth Collie and the Rough Collie are very similar, apart from their coat type, the Rough Collie obviously being the more demanding in this respect. Three colour varieties are recognized. These are the sable and white, which can vary from light gold to a rich shade of mahogany, the tri-colour, which is a combination of black, white and tan, especially on the head and legs, and the blue merle, which is silvery-blue, with black mixed in with the coloured hairs.

Collies have the typical characteristics of most sheep dogs. They are easy to train and delight in human company. They usually settle well as family pets, provided that they can have a run every day. They are loyal guards and prove wary of strangers.

DALMATIAN

ORIGINS	COAT TYPE/COLOUR
Yugoslavia	*short; black and white*
HEIGHT	**WEIGHT**
23–24 in (58.5–61 cm)	*55 lb (25 kg)*
CLASSIFICATION	
utility/non-sporting/companion	
NATURE	
energetic; good house dog	

It is believed that the English White Terrier, which has now vanished, was the main ancestor of this sturdy breed. Crossings involving Bulldogs, Dalmatians and others also played a part in its development. A dog dealer called James Hinks was instrumental in the early stages of its evolution, which took place in and around Birmingham, England. There was initial opposition from breeders of Staffordshire Bull Terriers, until one of Hinks's dogs beat a Staffordshire in a challenge dog fight so cleanly that it then won a dog show prize on the next day!

A miniature form, under 14 in (35 cm) in height, has since been developed, and both types are powerful, energetic dogs. They need firm training from an early age, especially to ensure that they will not fight with other dogs. The sheer power of the Bull Terrier makes it a formidable opponent, capable of inflicting serious injury. Nevertheless, they are normally quite trustworthy with people, although they will not tolerate intruders. It is best to avoid this breed if you have young children because these dogs are sometimes rather short-tempered.

COLLIE:
ROUGH AND SMOOTH

ORIGINS		COAT TYPE/COLOUR	
Scotland		*rough/flowing; wide variety*	
HEIGHT		**WEIGHT**	
22–24 in (56–61 cm); 18–19½ in (45.5–48.5 cm)		*45–65 lb (20.4–29.5 kg); 35–45 lb (13.6–20.4 kg)*	
CLASSIFICATION			
working/herding			
NATURE			
Strong-willed; requires much exercise			

This elegant breed was originally developed in Yugoslavia and subsequently brought to Britain where it became popular as a carriage dog during the eighteenth century, although its original function was probably to protect travellers against highwaymen. Dalmatians were also known for a time as 'firehouse dogs', because they used to accompany horse-drawn fire wagons through the streets of London.

These are very good house dogs and make dependable guardians. They are unlikely to bark unless there is a stranger in the vicinity. You must be willing to allow them a good run every day, however, which may not always be easy in a town. Dalmatians are energetic dogs by nature. Interestingly, their puppies are born pure white in colour and only develop their characteristic spots during the first few weeks of life. The short coat itself requires very little attention, even during a moult.

Check that any puppy that you are thinking of purchasing has normal hearing, as some individuals can prove deaf. In a good exhibition dog, the spots should be clearly defined and circular in shape. Although black-spotted Dalmatians are most common, there is also a variety with spots that are liver-brown in colour. The coat itself needs the minimum of grooming to stay in good condition, but, particularly during a moult, brushing should be carried out in the garden to save loose hairs from being shed around the home.

ELKHOUND
(NORWEGIAN ELKHOUND)

ORIGINS	COAT TYPE/COLOUR
Norway	*fluffy; grey/black*
HEIGHT	**WEIGHT**
20½ in (52 cm)	*50 lb (22.7 kg)*
CLASSIFICATION	
hound/large hound	
NATURE	
tough, devoted	

For many years, following its introduction to Britain in 1860 up until the First World War, the Flat-coated was the most popular of all retriever breeds. Subsequently, the essentially more colourful Golden and Labrador Retrievers took over this role, as the great estates with their gamekeepers broke up and the dog fancy developed to cater for the tastes of the exhibitor and pet-seeker. Originally known as the Wavy-coated Retriever, the inclusion of setters in the breeding gave rise to the coat type associated with this breed today.

The breed has undergone something of a revival, however, and achieved the Best in Show award at Crufts in 1980. As could be expected, these are hardy dogs and very responsive to training. They can make good house pets, but require a good period of exercise every day, which is easier to provide in rural surroundings. Their distinctive coat is relatively easy to keep in top condition through brushing. In terms of coloration, the Flat-coated Retriever is either a glossy black or liver, with no white markings being permitted.

GOLDEN RETRIEVER

ORIGINS	COAT TYPE/COLOUR
Scotland	*glossy; golden*
HEIGHT	**WEIGHT**
22–24 in (56–61 cm)	*70–80 lb (31.8–36.3 kg)*
CLASSIFICATION	
gundog/sporting	
NATURE	
delightful; excellent family dog	

Sometimes known also as the Norwegian Elkhound, especially in the United States, these ancient Nordic dogs were originally bred to track elk and other large animals, including bears, wolves and lynx. Within Scandinavia, there were several slightly different types, some of which were also used to pull sleighs. Instead of simply locating quarry, these dogs actually sought to drive it towards the hunter, which called for a considerable degree of courage.

Elkhounds were shown for the first time in 1877, at a gathering organized by the Norwegian Hunters' Association. They have remained tough, hardy dogs and make devoted companions. An active breed, Elkhounds require plenty of exercise and can be trained quite easily. There is a slight discrepancy in their classification, however, because the European canine authority, known as the Fédération Cynologique Internationale (FCI) distinguishes between the Norwegian Elkhound, which is grey in colour, and a slightly smaller form, known as the Black Norwegian Elkhound. Furthermore, a breed called the Jämthund or Swedish Elkhound is also recognized by the same organization.

FLAT-COATED RETRIEVER

ORIGINS	COAT TYPE/COLOUR
Newfoundland	*glossy; black/liver*
HEIGHT	**WEIGHT**
22–23 in (56–58.5 cm)	*60–70 lb (27.2–31.8 kg)*
CLASSIFICATION	
gundog/sporting	
NATURE	
hardy; very responsive to training	

These attractive dogs were another of the sporting breeds developed in the second half of the nineteenth century. They were bred on the Guisachan Estate in Scotland, which was owned by Lord Tweedmouth. Here the Golden Retriever initially evolved from crossing a yellow retriever of Flat-coat ancestry with a local and now extinct breed known as the Tweed Water Spaniel, itself a retriever with a tightly-curled coat. Detailed contemporary records show how the Golden Retriever came into existence over the course of the next two decades. There was introduction of new blood from further Labradors and Wavy-coated Retrievers as well as an Irish Setter. The Yellow or Golden Retriever, as the breed became known, rapidly gained in popularity in late-Victorian England.

At the turn of the century, the emergent breed was known as the Golden Flat-coated Retriever, and only achieved separate status in 1913. These dogs were already known in the United States by this stage, having been introduced here during the 1890s. There is still variation in the depth of coloration of the Golden Retriever. It can vary from cream to gold, but must not border on red or mahogany.

Goldren Retrievers are delightful dogs with an excellent temperament both as a gundog or family pet. Their natural retrieving instincts mean that they should be given a ball or flying disc to chase when they are being exercised. A good daily run is essential, and they will benefit from being kept in an environment with a large garden.

HUNGARIAN VIZSLA (VIZSLA)

ORIGINS	COAT TYPE/COLOUR
Hungary	*short;* *brownish-gold*
HEIGHT	**WEIGHT**
22½–25 in (57–63.5 cm)	*48½–66 lb (22–30 kg)*
CLASSIFICATION	
gundog/sporting	
NATURE	
obedient, affectionate	

The stunning appearance of these gundogs ensured their popularity and has led to them often being described as Red Setters. It is not always appreciated, however, that Irish Setters do need a considerable amount of exercise and if frustrated in this regard, they are likely to run off on their own.

The breed evolved from a combination of various other setters, such as the English and Gordon, with certain spaniel breeds. These included the Irish Water and Springer Spaniels. Early in its development, white coloration was prominent in its coat, but this form then went into decline until very recently, when it was revived as the Irish Red and White Setter. They are now considered as two separate breeds, while sharing a common ancestry.

Irish Setters are very affectionate dogs, but may prove more difficult to train than some gundogs. They have very sensitive natures, however, and respond to sympathetic handling. Their coats are reasonably easy to keep in top condition by regular brushing. Mud can be combed out of their 'feathering' (fringes of longer hair on the legs and body, as well as on the ears and tail) with ease once it is dry.

IRISH WATER SPANIEL

ORIGINS	COAT TYPE/COLOUR
Ireland	*tightly curled;* *dark liver, purlish*
HEIGHT	**WEIGHT**
21–23 in (53.5–58.5 cm)	*55–60 lb (25–27.2 kg)*
CLASSIFICATION	
gundog/sporting	
NATURE	
powerful swimmer; lively, affectionate	

This is another of the ancient Hungarian breeds, which has become quite well known in the West since the 1930s. Emigrés leaving Hungary brought their dogs with them, and from this base contemporary bloodlines have evolved. The name 'Vizsla', under which they are known in the United States, translates as 'responsive and alert'. These characteristics were essential attributes for a gundog in an area where natural cover was minimal. Vizslas also needed considerable stamina and were used to working in hot conditions, performing effectively both as pointers and retrievers.

The breed is even-tempered and settles well in the home provided that it has adequate opportunity for exercise. Its sleek, short coat creates an elegant appearance, and can range in coloration from sandy-yellow to gold. A more recent introduction has been the Wire-haired form, created during the 1930s by crossings involving the German Wire-haired Pointer. Sometimes referred to by its native name of Drotszoru, this has proved a somewhat hardier dog, happy to retrieve ducks from freezing water. Their affectionate natures make them well worth considering as pets.

IRISH SETTER

ORIGINS	COAT TYPE/COLOUR
Ireland	*glossy;* *rich chestnut*
HEIGHT	**WEIGHT**
21–24 in (53.5–61 cm)	*40–55 lb (18.2–25 kg)*
CLASSIFICATION	
gundog/sporting	
NATURE	
very affectionate and sensitive, sometimes wayward	

This traditional Irish breed may have descended originally from stock that originated in Europe. There is a clear relationship between the Standard Poodle and this breed, and there are suggestions that the Portuguese Water Dog might also have played a role in its development. There used to be two forms of water dog in Ireland. The North Water Spaniel was the smaller variety, with a wavy coat that was two-coloured (parti-coloured), while the southern form had a curly coat and, over all, was more similar to the contemporary Irish Water Spaniel.

The coat of this breed remains a distinctive feature, being dark liver with a slight purplish hue and quite tightly curled over the body. The hair on the legs and also on the top of the head is more open, with the face and tail having conspicuously straight hair.

These spaniels are totally at home in water, being powerful swimmers and able to dive without hesitation. Their coat provides good insulation, and is water-repellant. The Irish Water Spaniel is not a particularly common breed, but is very responsive to training and makes a lively, intelligent companion. You may have to tolerate your pet from time to time plunging into a pond, however, if the opportunity presents itself.

KERRY BLUE TERRIER

ORIGINS	COAT TYPE/COLOUR
Ireland	*wiry;* *black-blue*

HEIGHT	WEIGHT
18–19 in (45.5–48.5 cm)	*33–37 lb (15–16.8 kg)*

CLASSIFICATION	
terrier	

NATURE	
lively, affectionate; sometimes aggressive to other dogs	

Developed in the vicinity of County Kerry in southern Ireland well over a hundred years ago, this breed shows a clear resemblance to the Bedlington Terrier, which contributed to its ancestry. The Irish Terrier was also used in the development of the Kerry Blue Terrier, as is clearly evident from the the shape of the ears, which fall forward onto the forehead. These terriers were used originally to hunt a variety of creatures, notably foxes, badgers and otters, but since then, and especially in the 1920s, they became fashionable show dogs.

The coat of the Kerry Blue tends to be soft and wavy. Puppies are born black and their coats will lighten to blue by 18 months old, although they may still retain black points. Interestingly, those puppies whose coloration changes relatively late often have an adult coat that is a more desirable, darker shade of blue.

The Kerry Blue Terrier is a lively breed that does not always agree well with other dogs, although it should develop into an affectionate pet. It will also prove an alert guard dog and a keen rat-catcher. In Eire itself the breed is shown without any trimming, whereas elsewhere the coat is carefully groomed for the show ring.

LABRADOR RETRIEVER

ORIGINS	COAT TYPE/COLOUR
Newfoundland	*glossy;* *golden/black/chocolate*
HEIGHT	**WEIGHT**
22–22½ in (56–57 cm)	*55–57 lb (25–34 kg)*
CLASSIFICATION	
gundog/sporting	
NATURE	
trustworthy, active, affectionate	

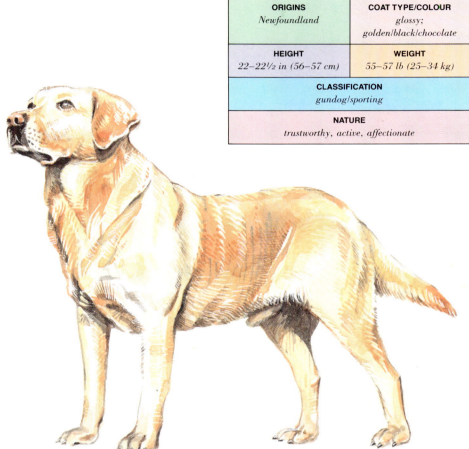

The ancestors of this well-known breed were brought originally from Newfoundland by fishermen returning to England. In Newfoundland the dogs helped to haul in the nets and took to the water readily. During the nineteenth century, a tax on dog ownership led to the demise of these dogs in Newfoundland, and British quarantine laws limited the availability of further stock. They were then interbred with existing retriever breeds such as the Flat-coated until finally, in 1903, a standard was established for the Labrador Retriever itself.

Since then, these dogs have undergone a massive surge in popularity, being kept both as house pets and gundogs. They have retained their affiliation with water and are highly valued by duck hunters. Their scenting skills have also been exploited in other areas of contemporary life, including the search for drugs and explosives at airports. The trustworthy nature of the Labrador Retriever has also seen the breed trained as guide dogs for people with impaired sight.

In terms of coloration, although the black form was best known during the early years of the century, the yellow variety is now more common. Chocolate individuals may also be seen occasionally as well. It is not unusual for the coat coloration of yellow Labradors to fade somewhat with age, although there is a natural variation to some extent in any event.

In the case of black and chocolate dogs, the development of some white hairs around the muzzle can be anticipated as they become older. These are not sedentary dogs by nature, and you must be prepared to give them plenty of exercise, because otherwise they will rapidly become obese.

SIBERIAN HUSKY

ORIGINS	COAT TYPE/COLOUR
Siberia	*fluffy; wide variety*

HEIGHT	WEIGHT
21–23½ in (53.5–59.5 cm)	*45–60 lb (20.4–27.2 kg)*

CLASSIFICATION	
working/guard	

NATURE	
bold, lively, friendly; great stamina	

The precise origins of this breed, which resembles the Brittany, are unclear. It may have resulted from the combination of English Springers and Clumber Spaniels, but the only accepted colour combination is rich red and white. Welsh Springers were recognized officially by the Kennel Club in 1902, but are not a very common breed, although they are widely known and are accepted by the American Kennel Club. Welsh Springers are quite easy to prepare for showing. Their coats are relatively soft and any sign of curling is considered a distinct fault.

These spaniels have great stamina and prove diligent workers, not afraid of entering water. As a result, they are not well suited to a purely domestic existence, but will thrive here if they are also kept active. They prove loyal and trustworthy dogs, with a keen scenting ability, like their English counterparts.

WIRE-HAIRED POINTING GRIFFON

ORIGINS	COAT TYPE/COLOUR
?France	*wiry; chestnut and white*

HEIGHT	WEIGHT
21½–23½ in (54.5–59.5 cm)	*50–60 lb (22.7–27.2 kg)*

CLASSIFICATION	
sporting/gundog	

NATURE	
dedicated, hard-working, loyal	

Few dogs have more stamina than the Siberian Husky, which was developed as a sleigh dog by the Chukchi tribe who lived in north-east Asia. From here, some of these dogs were taken to Alaska just after the turn of the present century, where they won the gruelling 400-mile (644-km) All Alaska Sweepstake Race. The popularity of these dogs spread, helped by their appealing temperament.

In addition to being kept just as active companions or show dogs, however, they have also been used in recent years to develop the sport of sled racing. This is now a popular pursuit among owners of these Huskies, both in the United States and in parts of Europe, including Britain. There are no restrictions on the coloration of the Siberian Husky, and some individuals are most attractively marked. They are also known under the alternative name of Arctic Husky.

WELSH SPRINGER SPANIEL

ORIGINS		COAT TYPE/COLOUR
?Great Britain		*silky; rich red and white*
HEIGHT		**WEIGHT**
19 in (48.5 cm)		*35–45 lb (15.9–20.4 kg)*
CLASSIFICATION		
gundog/sporting		
NATURE		
hard-working; difficult to train; versatile		

This breed of gundog was developed originally by a Dutch enthusiast called Edward Korthals, who started his quest in 1874. Unfortunately, a clear picture of its ancestry is not available, although it is known that Korthals began with a grey and brown Griffon bitch and, apart from other Griffons, various setters and pointers may also have been used. For part of the time, Korthals worked in France for the Duke of Penthièvre, and so this country is officially listed as the homeland of the Wire-haired Pointing Griffon.

This new breed was being shown in 1888 in Britain, but has since faded from the scene here, although it is recognized by both the American and Canadian Kennel Clubs. Even so, it is scarce in these countries, being concentrated in the hands of a few breeders and used mainly for working rather than show purposes. The Wire-haired Pointing Griffon is relatively slow in the field, but possesses a keen nose. It is a tough breed, with its hard coat offering good protection in marshy surroundings, and it can also swim if necessary. It is either solid chestnut in colour, or chestnut with steel-grey or white markings. These are dogs that need plenty of exercise, and that establish a strong bond with their owners.

4
LARGE BREEDS
DOGS BETWEEN 24 AND 30 in (60–76 cm)

Here can be found some of the most popular hounds, as well as various guard dogs, which, in view of their size and naturally dominant natures, are perhaps not the best choice for a novice owner. All dogs need to be trained properly, however, and to seek help in this area you can attend a local training group run under the guidance of an expert tutor. Ask at your public library or your veterinary surgery for details of courses near you.

AFGHAN HOUND

ORIGINS	COAT TYPE/COLOUR
Afghanistan	*flowing; wide variety*
HEIGHT	**WEIGHT**
20–27 in (51–68.5 cm)	*77–88 lb (35–40 kg)*
CLASSIFICATION	
hound/coursing	
NATURE	
destructive if under-exercised; devoted and friendly	

The loyalty of the Akita is legendary in its Japanese homeland. A dog called Hachiko used to walk back and forth to a railway station near Tokyo with its owner every day. When the man died at work, the Akita continued its daily journey for the remainder of its life, in the hope that one day its master would return. On Hachiko's demise, a statue was erected in his memory, with the Akita itself being declared a 'national monument' in Japan. This ensures that financial support is available for people who may no longer be able to afford to care for a breed champion.

The Akita's origins date back to the seventeenth century. It was first bred in the province of Akita, located on the island of Honshu, from spitz stock. They were developed as hunting dogs and trained to work in pairs. Akitas started to become popular in the United States during the 1950s, with a specialist breed club being founded here in 1956. They have also gained a strong following in Britain during recent years.

Akitas (which resemble Chow Chows, to a certain extent) are very powerful dogs with a stubborn streak and therefore they must be properly trained, otherwise the slightly dominant and aggressive streak in their natures can become evident. They will be content with a good walk every day, and their coat is easy to keep in condition by regular brushing.

ALASKAN MALAMUTE

ORIGINS	COAT TYPE/COLOUR
Alaska, United States	*fluffy; black (or grey) and white*
HEIGHT	**WEIGHT**
25–28 in (63.5–71 cm)	*85–125 lb (37.8–55.6 kg)*
CLASSIFICATION	
working/guard	
NATURE	
good companion; hardy	

As a sight hound, this can prove one of the most difficult breeds to train to return to you. Afghans were originally bred to hunt hares, deer and even wolves in Afghanistan. The Afghan is not a pack hound and is used to working on its own, in conjunction with a horse and rider. Hunting over the inhospitable rocky terrain called for a breed with plenty of stamina and keen eyesight.

The Afghan Hound was first brought to Britain at the end of the nineteenth century, by soldiers coming home from the Afghan War. Serious interest in these hounds led to the formation of a breed club in 1926. Within Afghanistan, there were several different forms, some of which were bigger and had darker coats than others. These distinctions remained noticeable in the early Afghan bloodlines, but have now essentially disappeared. Their coat does appear to have become more profuse, however, and this aristocratic hound needs thorough daily grooming to prevent its hair from becoming matted. Air-cushioned brushes are often recommended for this purpose.

Sadly, the graceful elegance of the Afghan has attracted owners who have neither the time nor space needed for this breed. These hounds must have a good run off the lead every day, preferably away from areas where other smaller dogs are exercised, otherwise these may be chased. Afghans will amply reward the efforts of their owner, proving both affectionate and devoted, but are soon likely to turn destructive if they are bored.

AKITA

ORIGINS		COAT TYPE/COLOUR	
Japan		*fluffy; wide variety*	
HEIGHT		WEIGHT	
20–27 in (51–68.5 cm)		*77–88 lb (35–40 kg)*	
CLASSIFICATION			
working/guard			
NATURE			
very powerful, slightly stubborn			

This is one of the native North American spitz breeds, developed by a tribe called the Mahlemuts, after which they are named. Alaskan Malamutes are used in sleigh teams, and six harnessed together can cover a distance of 50 miles (80 km) in a day, pulling loads of 700 lb (355 kg) or more. Their rather vulpine appearance belies an affectionate nature. They tend to be a combination of grey or black and white, with distinctive facial patterning forming a mask or cap, or a combination of both.

As may be anticipated from their origins, these are active dogs, not suited to apartment living. At present, the Alaskan Malamute may be less common than other similar breeds such as the Siberian Husky, but it appears to be growing in popularity, especially in the United States and Canada. Coat care presents no particular problems and they are, in addition, very hardy dogs, able to live outdoors in kennels if required, although they do delight in human companionship.

BELGIAN SHEPHERD DOGS: GROENENDAEL (BELGIAN SHEEPDOG), LAEKENOIS, MALINOIS, TERVUEREN

ORIGINS	COAT TYPE/COLOUR
Belgium	*smooth/shaggy; wide variety*
HEIGHT	**WEIGHT**
24–26 in (61–66 cm)	*62 lb (28.1 kg)*
CLASSIFICATION	
working/herding	
NATURE	
adjust well to home environment; wary of strangers	

The ancestry of this old Swiss breed may date back over 2,000 years to the days of the Roman Empire. Similar dogs were probably developed in Switzerland to protect supply lines as the empire expanded. The fortunes of the breed declined during the latter part of the last century, however, until a group of breeders sought out the few remaining dogs and managed to ensure their survival.

Out of the four breeds of Swiss Mountain Dogs, the Bernese can be easily distinguished by virtue of its long, silky coat, whereas the coats of the others are short. All are similar in coloration, being a combination of black with white on the head, chest and toes, and intervening areas of rich tan on the legs, chest and cheeks. The coat is easy to keep in good condition and benefits from daily brushing.

Bernese Mountain Dogs are loyal and alert guard dogs, with a sound temperament that makes them suitable as family pets. They are active and need plenty of exercise, otherwise they can start to put on weight and are liable to become bored.

BLOODHOUND

ORIGINS	COAT TYPE/COLOUR
the Holy Land	*short; wide variety*
HEIGHT	**WEIGHT**
25–27 in (63.5–68.5 cm)	*88 lb (40 kg)*
CLASSIFICATION	
hound/large hound	
NATURE	
sensitive, friendly; requires long walks	

Sometimes known as sheepdogs, these dogs were developed both as guard dogs and for herding purposes. Similar dogs have been kept in Belgium since the Middle Ages, but no serious attempt was made to classify them until 1891. At that stage, eight different breeds were distinguished, but now just four remain.

The Groenendael, with its long black coat, is the form often described in the United States simply as the Belgian Sheepdog. They were introduced here for the first time in 1907, and were also used in the First World War, both as messengers and sentries.

The Tervueren is quite similar to the Groenendael, but can be distinguished by its coloration, which ranges from fawn to mahogany, with the individual hairs themselves being tipped with black. These darker markings are most prominent on the head, forequarters and at the tip of the tail.

The smooth-coated Malinois is rather reminiscent of a German Shepherd Dog (formerly called the Alsatian). It was originally developed in the area around Malines, as a sheep-herder. Like their German counterparts, these dogs are very responsive to training. They are likely to prove protective towards their owners and are reluctant to accept strangers.

The final variety of the Belgian Shepherd is the Laekenois, which was first bred in the vicinity of Boom in Antwerp. Here it served to guard linen that was left to bleach in the sun. The Laekenois is fawn in coloration, with black markings confined to the face.

BERNESE MOUNTAIN DOG

ORIGINS	COAT TYPE/COLOUR
Switzerland	*long, silky; black, white and tan*

HEIGHT	WEIGHT
25–27½ in (63.5–70 cm)	*88 lb (40 kg)*

CLASSIFICATION
working/guard

NATURE
sound temperament; loyal and alert

Known for its scenting skills, the Bloodhound was probably developed from an old breed known as the St Hubert Hound, which was brought to Europe by soldiers returning from the Crusades before the Middle Ages. It was introduced to Britain by the Normans after the Battle of Hastings in 1066. As a result of the careful breeding of these hounds, they became known as 'blooded hounds', which, in turn, was presumably shortened simply to Bloodhound.

In spite of their name, these are not aggressive dogs and make good family pets. They will need long walks, however, where their scenting skills will soon become apparent. Bloodhounds are surprisingly sensitive by nature and respond best to encouragement rather than criticism. You will need to watch their pendulous ears, as these are easily damaged. Their eyes, too, can suffer from problems, while the wrinkled skin on their head may provide a focus for local infections. Bloodhounds usually prove hardy and tenacious by nature. They are bred in several colours, notably combinations of black and tan and liver and tan, as well as red. Small areas of white on the chest, feet and at the tip of the tail will not be penalized for show purposes.

BORZOI

ORIGINS	COAT TYPE/COLOUR
Soviet Union	*silky;* *generally whitish*

HEIGHT	WEIGHT
29 in (73.5 cm)	*75–105 lb (34–46.7 kg)*

CLASSIFICATION	
hound/coursing	

NATURE	
rather remote; requires room to run	

It may be that this breed originated in the French province of Brie as long ago as the twelfth century. Here it was valued as a guard dog, protecting sheep from wolves and other dangers, but, as wolves were gradually eliminated, it also served to herd farmstock. The Briard today has retained a brave nature, and will be alert to any intruders around your property. It is easily trained and will settle well in domestic surroundings, provided that it has plenty of opportunity to exercise every day.

The flowing coat of the Briard obviously needs daily brushing. An unusual feature laid down in the breed standard is that the double dew claws present on the hindlegs are retained.

Dew claws are normally removed from other breeds because they serve no real purpose for dogs today and there is a risk, especially with the front dew claws, that the dog could become caught up by them, resulting in injury. Where the dew claws are left, however, you may need to trim them regularly, because they will not become worn down in the normal fashion as they are not in contact with the ground. As a result, the claws are likely to become overgrown and will curl back or, even worse, can penetrate the dog's skin.

In spite of its long history, the Briard has only become more widely known outside France during recent years.

BULLMASTIFF

ORIGINS	COAT TYPE/COLOUR
England	*short;* *brindle/fawn/red*

HEIGHT	WEIGHT
25–27 in (63.5–68.5 cm)	*110–130 lb (50–59 kg)*

CLASSIFICATION	
working/guard	

NATURE	
powerful, affectionate; needs careful training	

Another member of the sight hounds, the Borzoi evolved in the Soviet Union to hunt wolves, and is sometimes also known as the Russian Wolfhound. It has an elegant, aristocratic appearance – long legs, a gracefully curving back with a long neck and tapering head – and appears to have changed little since it was developed in the middle of the seventeenth century. Borzois hunted in couples, approaching a wolf simultaneously from each side. They then wrestled it to the ground and held it for the huntsman so that it could be killed.

Borzois were first exhibited in Britain by the Prince of Wales at the end of the last century, and also became known in the United States at about the same time. In 1903 the Russian Wolfhound Club of America was founded and did much to popularize the breed. They can be bred in any colour, although white is generally prominent in their coat, which needs careful grooming to preserve its appearance.

Borzois can prove rather remote by nature, being far less playful than many other breeds. It is important that they be kept in an environment where they can use their speed regularly. There are few sights more graceful than these dogs running together.

BRIARD

ORIGINS	COAT TYPE/COLOUR
France	*flowing; generally black*
HEIGHT	**WEIGHT**
24–27 in (61–68.5 cm)	*75 lb (34 kg)*
CLASSIFICATION	
working/herding	
NATURE	
independent streak; very loyal	

This is a large and powerful breed that was developed by crossing the English Mastiff with the Bulldog. It was bred specifically to combat poachers on the large estates in Britain during the early 1800s. Being smaller than the original Mastiff, yet with the tenacity of the Bulldog, it was an agile and loyal companion for a solitary gamekeeper who might encounter a violent group of poachers.

Down the years, the temperament of the Bullmastiff has altered noticeably and they now prove affectionate family dogs, although it is essential that these dogs are properly trained to deter any lingering aggressive tendencies. Bullmastiffs are still powerful dogs, however, and are not suitable for a child to exercise. They have been bred in an attractive range of colours, with a slight white marking on the chest being acceptable, but not really desirable in a show dog. The mask is frequently black.

DOBERMANN
(DOBERMAN PINSCHER)

ORIGINS	COAT TYPE/COLOUR
Germany	*short; black (or brown) and tan*

HEIGHT	WEIGHT
27 in (68.5 cm)	*66–80 lb (30–36.3 kg)*

CLASSIFICATION	
working/guard	

NATURE	
needs firm training to curb aggressive tendencies	

The history of the English Setter dates back to about the middle of the nineteenth century, when, according to contemporary accounts, these dogs were developed from spaniels. The purpose of a setter was to locate game and then drop down to indicate its presence. The breed was first taken to the United States in 1874, and here they soon began to make a strong impression in field trials.

The English Setter is still highly valued as a gundog and can be trained quite easily for this purpose. These dogs enjoy an outdoor life and should never be kept in a small apartment, deprived of the opportunity for proper exercise. They have been bred in various colour combinations with white, including liver, lemon and black forms. There is also a tri-colour, which is black, white and tan.

Providing you have adequate space, this gentle and affectionate breed will be an ideal choice as a family pet, although the coat will require grooming and some trimming to maintain its good condition. It is customary to bathe these dogs prior to a show and then comb the coat flat while it is still wet, leaving it to dry in this position.

GERMAN POINTERS:
LONG-HAIRED,
SHORT-HAIRED AND
WIRE-HAIRED

ORIGINS	COAT TYPE/COLOUR
Germany	*long, short and wiry; wide variety*

HEIGHT	WEIGHT
24–25 in (61–63.5 cm)	*55–70 lb (25–31.2 kg)*

CLASSIFICATION	
gundog	

NATURE	
responsive to training	

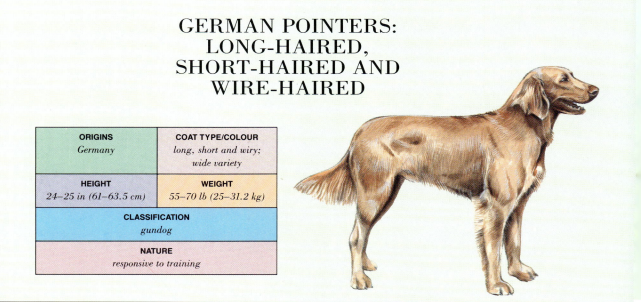

This breed is better known in North America as the Doberman Pinscher, with 'Doberman' in this case being spelt with a single 'n'. Its origins date back to 1870, when a German breeder called Louis Dobermann sought to develop a new breed, based largely on a combination of Rottweiler and German Pinscher blood. He wanted a breed that would protect him in his unpopular work as a tax collector. A variety of other dogs contributed to his breeding programme, including German Shepherd Dogs and probably Greyhounds, which helped to give the Dobermann its sleek appearance.

By the turn of the century, the Dobermann had gained a justifiable reputation for its aggressive behaviour. When the breed was introduced to the US, breeders in the UK realized that if it was to make progress in show circles, then a much more docile dog would be required. Its attractive profile helped to ensure the rapid rise in popularity of the Dobermann, both in North America and elsewhere, but bad publicity has tended to follow this breed.

Many problems can be traced back to early care. The Dobermann is naturally a very assertive dog and so must receive proper training from puppyhood, otherwise it may well turn aggressive in later life. For this reason, it is not the best breed to choose as a family pet, nor if you have had little or no previous experience of owning a dog. A well-trained and obedient Dobermann is, nevertheless, a joy to watch, and the breed is used by police forces in various countries.

ENGLISH SETTER

ORIGINS	COAT TYPE/COLOUR
England	*silky;* *wide variety*
HEIGHT	**WEIGHT**
25–27 in (63.5–68.5 cm)	*66 lb (30 kg)*
CLASSIFICATION	
gundog/sporting	
NATURE	
an 'outdoor' dog; gentle and affectionate	

The various breeds of German Pointer are closely related. The Short-haired form is the most common and is considered to be one of the best sporting dogs. It can work both as a pointer, indicating the presence of game, and as a retriever, while it is equally versatile on land or water. This breed has a mixed ancestry, which involved the Spanish Pointer, a number of native hounds and possibly the English form of the Pointer as well.

In turn, the German Short-haired Pointer contributed to the development of the Wire-haired form, known also as the Drahthaar. Its wiry coat affords good protection in undergrowth, while the dense undercoat is shed during the warmer summer months. German Pointers have all the usual attributes of gundogs, not least being the fact that they are responsive to training, although the Drahthaar may be slightly more difficult in this respect.

The German Long-haired Pointer or Langhaar has become quite scarce. This breed was used originally for falconry purposes. Its decline has been linked to the rising popularity of the Wire-haired form, and possibly its duller coloration has also counted against it. These pointers are either light brown or a dead-leaf shade, whereas greater variety is seen in the German Wire-haired, with liver and white combinations being common.

GIANT SCHNAUZER

ORIGINS	COAT TYPE/COLOUR
Germany	*wiry;* *black/pepper and salt*
HEIGHT	**WEIGHT**
25½–27½ in (65–75 cm)	*77 lb (35 kg)*
CLASSIFICATION	
utility/working/guard	
NATURE	
powerful, lively; wary of strangers	

The well-muscled profile of the Greyhound reveals a breed that has been bred for its pace. Illustrations of dogs of this type can be found on ancient Egyptian tombs dating back over 5,000 years. They were certainly known in Britain by the 900s, and were jealously guarded by the nobility here, to prevent poaching activities. In more recent times, Greyhound racing has become a popular sport in many countries. Dogs that are retired from the track, often by four years old, can settle well as household pets, although they should be muzzled when they are first let off the leash, otherwise they may pursue a toy breed or cat with fatal consequences. In terms of temperament, Greyhounds are very gentle dogs and particularly tolerant with children.

A short brisk run will suit them well in terms of exercise, and their short coat is easy to groom. Greyhounds are not guard dogs in any sense, however, and rarely bark in domestic surroundings. An unusual feature of this breed is that it is not troubled by hip dysplasia, unlike most other larger breeds of dog.

IBIZAN HOUND

ORIGINS	COAT TYPE/COLOUR
Ibiza	*short;* *wide variety*
HEIGHT	**WEIGHT**
22–29 in (56–73.5 cm)	*42–50 lb (19–22.7 kg)*
CLASSIFICATION	
hound/coursing	
NATURE	
receptive to domestic life; needs much exercise	

Another German breed, the Giant Schnauzer arose in the south of the country and was used in Britain for herding cattle. They have also been used as police dogs. Giant Schnauzers are now often less popular than the Miniature and Standard forms (see page 48), which they otherwise resemble in terms of care. These dogs are frequently pure black in colour, but may also be seen in shades of pepper and salt, in equal proportions in the case of a show dog.

Coat care of Schnauzers may prove quite demanding, with their whiskers and moustache requiring to be combed each day. In addition, stripping the coat will also be necessary at regular intervals, although you can have this carried out professionally at a grooming parlour if so desired.

GREYHOUND

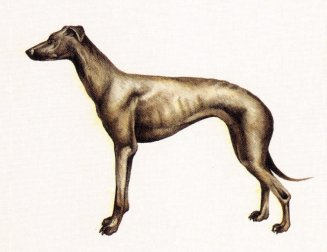

ORIGINS		COAT TYPE/COLOUR	
?Egypt		*short;* *wide variety*	
HEIGHT		**WEIGHT**	
28–30 in (71–76 cm)		*60–70 lb (27.2–31.8 kg)*	
CLASSIFICATION			
hound/coursing			
NATURE			
very gentle, affectionate; requires wide spaces			

This appears to be another ancient breed, which was known to the Egyptians. Its modern name is derived from the island of Ibiza, where the breed is believed to have been maintained in a virtually pure state for several thousand years. Ibizan Hounds are also traditionally popular in nearby Spain, where a wire-haired version is known. These hounds have only become known to a wider audience during recent years, however, first reaching the United States in 1956.

Their sleek, alert demeanour has ensured that they have established a strong following. Their hearing is acute, and they are now valued as gundogs. Ibizan Hounds will settle easily in domestic surroundings, getting along well with children, and are not aggressive by nature. You will need to be prepared to take considerable exercise, however, if you decide to keep one of these lively hounds. They can be either a solid red, white or lion (tawny), but are more often a combination of these colours.

NEAPOLITAN MASTIFF

ORIGINS	COAT TYPE/COLOUR
Italy	*short; grey/black*
HEIGHT	**WEIGHT**
25–29 in (63.5–73.5 cm)	*up to 155 lb (69 kg)*
CLASSIFICATION	
guard	
NATURE	
agreeable; requires much exercise	

Two different forms of dog developed in Newfoundland, descended from European varieties brought by sailors. While the smaller form was to become the ancestor of the Labrador Retriever, the Greater St John's Dog evolved into the breed that is recognized today as the Newfoundland. These dogs took to water readily and, because of their size and strength, were able to save the lives of drowning sailors.

The Newfoundland was first brought to Britain during 1860, but subsequently had nearly died out by the end of the Second World War. Many of today's bloodlines can be traced back to later imports of American dogs, which main-tained the breed's existence in Britain. Both black and brown forms are now recognized, as well as a white and black form that is known as the Landseer after the famous Victorian artist Sir Edwin Landseer (1802–73), who painted these dogs.

Newfoundlands are well-balanced, amenable dogs that will settle well in a household large enough to accommodate them. They have retained their swimming skills, and can also prove valuable as guard dogs. Their size alone is a considerable deterrent, but if threatened, they are likely to prove fierce in defence of people around them.

PHARAOH HOUND

ORIGINS	COAT TYPE/COLOUR
Malta	*sleek, short; reddish-tan*
HEIGHT	**WEIGHT**
22–25 in (56–63.5 cm)	*65 lb (29.5 kg)*
CLASSIFICATION	
hound/coursing	
NATURE	
friendly; requires much exercise	

The origins of this Italian mastiff stretch right back to the fierce Molossus dogs of ancient Rome. These mastiffs have particularly large heads, supported by equally powerful bodies. They used to be concentrated largely in their Italian homeland, but are now being seen in greater numbers elsewhere. Neapolitan Mastiffs are bred in shades of grey and black. Although used for dog-fighting in the past, they generally prove quite tolerant dogs. Nevertheless, they retain strong territorial instincts and will prove determined guards.

NEWFOUNDLAND

ORIGINS *Newfoundland*	COAT TYPE/COLOUR *coarse, dense; black/ brown/black and white*
HEIGHT *28 in (71 cm)*	WEIGHT *140–150 lb (63.4–68 kg)*
CLASSIFICATION *working/guard*	
NATURE *powerful, amenable, well-balanced; good swimmer*	

The Phoenicians are believed to have brought these hounds to the islands of Malta and Gozo over 5,000 years ago, and, since then, the breed has developed largely in isolation. They are popular here for hunting rabbits and, although sight hounds, they can also track their quarry by scent.

There are obvious similarities in appearance between the Pharaoh and Ibizan Hounds, but their coloration is different. Pharaoh Hounds are tan or rich tan, and chestnut forms may also be recognized. A white tip to the tail is encouraged, and a white area on the chest, known as the star, with other white areas on the toes and a narrow blaze down the centre of the nose are also allowed for show purposes. The temperament of both breeds is alike, with the Pharaoh Hound benefiting from a good daily run. The rise in popularity of the Pharaoh Hound has been quite staggering. Back in 1970, none were registered with the Kennel Club, yet within five years, they were given championship status. A similar occurrence took place in North America.

POINTER

ORIGINS	COAT TYPE/COLOUR
?Spain	*short;* *wide variety*
HEIGHT	**WEIGHT**
25–27 in (63.5–68.5 cm)	*44–66 lb (20–30 kg)*
CLASSIFICATION	
gundog/sporting/companion	
NATURE	
essentially a working dog, but can settle well in the home	

Better known in North America simply as the Great Pyrenees, these large shepherd dogs were bred from mastiff stock and served to protect sheep from wolves, being equipped with fearsome spiked collars to defend themselves. Later they were used to smuggle contraband across the steep mountain paths that separated France and Spain, being fitted with special satchels for this purpose.

The breed had declined sharply by the turn of the century, and could have died out, but then a breeding programme was launched in which emphasis was placed on producing dogs that were good-natured, lacking the traditional aggressive traits. This has been successfully achieved, although these dogs still show a marked reluctance to accept strangers and will prove alert guard dogs.

In a show ring, these predominantly white dogs are an impressive sight. They were first recognized by the American Kennel Club in 1933, before being accepted by the British organization 11 years later. The double dew claws on the hindfeet are deemed a breed characteristic and should never be removed in show dogs.

RHODESIAN RIDGEBACK

ORIGINS	COAT TYPE/COLOUR
South Africa	*short;* *wheaten*
HEIGHT	**WEIGHT**
25–27 in (63.5–68.5 cm)	*75–85 lb (34–38.6 kg)*
CLASSIFICATION	
hound/small hound	
NATURE	
enjoys human company; intolerant of trespassers	

The original purpose of the Pointer was to find and indicate a 'point' where hares were lurking, so that Greyhounds could then be brought in to run them down. The advent of shooting, however, saw the role of the Pointer modified to finding suitable game for the guns. Pointers are therefore essentially working dogs, but can settle in the home if they have plenty of exercise as well.

The influence of the Pointer (its 'frozen' stance characteristic of its field work) has extended into many other contemporary gun-dogs, although its origins are now unclear. It has been suggested that it may first have been bred in Spain, using a combination of Bloodhounds, Greyhounds and Foxhounds. The Spanish Pointer is a heavier breed today than its English counterpart, which is the form known simply as the Pointer. It is bred in a variety of colours, including lemon, orange and black and liver, as well as combined forms with white. Tricoloured forms are also known.

PYRENEAN MOUNTAIN DOG (GREAT PYRENEES)

ORIGINS		COAT TYPE/COLOUR	
the Pyrenees		*thick, shaggy; generally white*	
HEIGHT		**WEIGHT**	
28 in + (71 cm)		*110 lb + (50 kg)*	
CLASSIFICATION			
working/herding			
NATURE			
good-natured, though wary with strangers			

The unusual name of this breed is derived from the raised line of hair along its back, which forms two whorls or crowns just behind the shoulders. The Rhodesian Ridgeback evolved in southern Africa, and this characteristic pattern reflects an ancestry that extends back to an old breed known as the African Hottentot Hunting Dog. The Ridgeback was bred by European settlers who were seeking a dog that could survive in the harsh and often inhospitable African climate. For a period, they were used to hunt lions, and so became known as the African Lion Hound.

Rhodesian Ridgebacks enjoy human company and are affectionate by nature, but they will not tolerate trespassers on their property. Although not common, the breed still enjoys a dedicated following. These are truly unusual dogs with an interesting history, and while they may sleep longer than other breeds, Rhodesian Ridgebacks will spark into life when out for a run. They are an attractive shade of wheaten colour, and may also show traces of white on their chest and toes.

ROTTWEILER

ORIGINS	COAT TYPE/COLOUR
Germany	*short;*
	black and tan

HEIGHT	WEIGHT
25–27 in (63.5–68.5 cm)	*110 lb (50 kg)*

CLASSIFICATION
working/guard

NATURE
potentially temperamental; unsuitable as family dog

The origins of this Swiss breed can be traced to the Hospice du Grand St Bernard, at St Gotthard's Pass, located high in the Alps close to the Italian border. Strong and courageous by nature (though, sadly, rather short-lived), these large dogs were used to rescue stranded travellers. Around their necks, attached to the collar, hung a small keg of medicinal brandy that was used to revive people dug out of the snow. An individual St Bernard was said to have saved the lives of 40 people during the first 10 years of the nineteenth century.

The breed declined badly soon afterwards, and crosses with Newfoundlands were used in an attempt to revive it. The St Bernard was finally shown for the first time in Britain in 1866, and these dogs were taken to the United States four years later. Their large size gives them correspondingly healthy appetites, and they can cause problems for house-proud owners by drooling around the home. The St Bernard remains one of the most intelligent and affectionate breeds, but it can suffer badly from hind-limb weaknesses.

SALUKI

ORIGINS	COAT TYPE/COLOUR
Middle East	*silky;*
	wide variety

HEIGHT	WEIGHT
23–28 in (55.5–71 cm)	*66 lb max (30 kg)*

CLASSIFICATION
working/guard

NATURE
loyal; requires considerable exercise

During recent years, the popularity of the Rottweiler has grown at a tremendous rate. Unfortunately, a number of people have been attracted to this dog because of its macho image and, sadly, serious and sometimes fatal injuries have been caused by Rottweilers going beserk, frequently because of poor training. This is actually an intelligent and responsive breed, which has been used for a wide variety of purposes, ranging from police dogs to mountain rescue guides. It is also a prominent contender in many obedience competitions, and a popular entrant in the show ring.

Rottweilers were unknown in Britain until 1936, having been recognized only the previous year by the American Kennel Club. The breed's origins can be traced back to the town of Rott-weil in Württemberg, Germany. Their ancestors were used to drive cattle to market and to guard them. In addition, they were trained to pull carts and defend their owners from attacks by highwaymen.

The Rottweiler is not a breed that can be recommended for a home where there are young children. Firm training is also essential, and you must spend sufficient time with these dogs to ensure that they do not become bored, as this can be a recipe for disaster. Exercise is also essential, and it may be worth fitting a muzzle to your pet when it is off the leash, especially in the company of other dogs. Even fellow dog-owners may be nervous about Rottweilers, following the unwelcome publicity that the breed has generated.

ST BERNARD

ORIGINS	COAT TYPE/COLOUR
Switzerland	*shaggy; black, cream and wheaten*
HEIGHT	**WEIGHT**
27½ in (70 cm)	*110–121 lb (50–54.9 kg)*
CLASSIFICATION	
working/guard	
NATURE	
friendly, affable; requires considerable household space	

These athletic sight hounds were originally developed in the Middle East and are of ancient lineage. Dogs of similar appearance were being kept in this region over 2,000 years ago, and were used to hunt gazelles, which rank among the fastest of all antelope. When they were first seen in Britain, about 1840, they were described as Persian Greyhounds, having originated from Persia (modern-day Iran). They only became widely available at the turn of the century, and were recognized by the Kennel Club in 1922, and by the American Kennel Club five years later.

These hounds make loyal companions, but should only be kept if you can give them plenty of exercise. Salukis may need to be supervised closely when they are off the leash, because they have not lost their hunting instincts. Available in a good choice of colours, daily brushing of the Saluki's coat is essential to maintain its sleek appearance. You may need to comb the longer hair on the ears and tail.

TIBETAN MASTIFF

ORIGINS	COAT TYPE/COLOUR
Tibet	*shaggy; black and tan/golden*

HEIGHT	WEIGHT
24–27 in (61–68.5 cm)	*220 lb (97.9 kg)*

CLASSIFICATION	
guard	

NATURE	
hardy, obedient; OK with children	

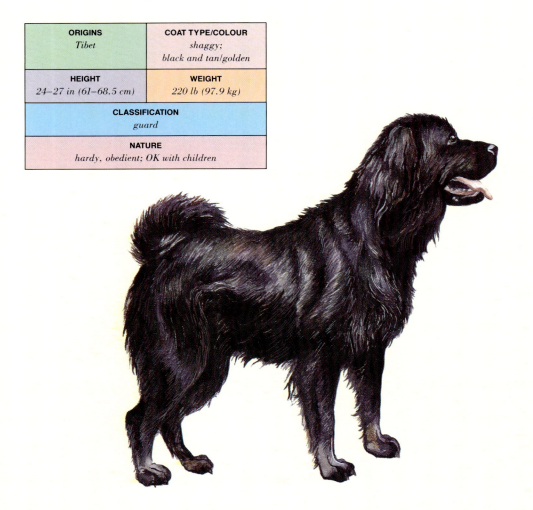

These large dogs bear some similarity to the St Bernard, although they were developed far away in Tibet. In their homeland, Tibetan Mastiffs were used to guard and herd flocks. They may be the closest surviving relative of the original ancestral form of the many mastiff breeds, which is thought to have been developed in this area.

Unlike some of the smaller Tibetan dogs, however, this mastiff has never been well known outside its homeland, although it did have a brief period of popularity in Britain during the last century. King George IV (1762–1830) kept two of these dogs, and the Prince of Wales (later King Edward VII) exhibited the breed in 1875. The black and tan or golden forms are best known in the West, but pure black dogs, some showing white markings, have been recorded in Tibet.

There are now signs that Tibetan Mastiffs are becoming more popular. They are hardy and essentially obedient dogs, which can generally be trusted with children in spite of their large size. The American Tibetan Mastiff Association is working hard to encourage the development of this breed along correct lines, ensuring both genetic and temperamental soundness. Interestingly, bitches only come into season once a year rather than twice as most other breeds do.

WEIMARANER

ORIGINS	COAT TYPE/COLOUR
Germany	*sleek;* *silver-grey*
HEIGHT	**WEIGHT**
24–27 in (61–68.5 cm)	*70–85 lb (31.8–38.6 kg)*
CLASSIFICATION	
gundog/sporting	
NATURE	
obedient and loyal	

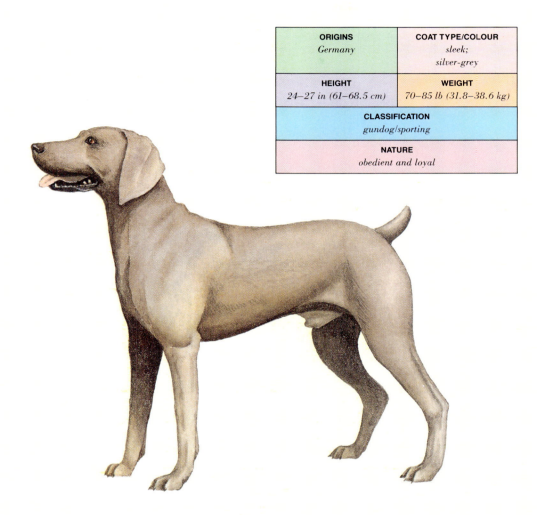

This breed has been developed with considerable care. It originated in Germany during the last century, from crossings of various breeds, including pointers, and was bred as a gundog. The German breed club insisted on rigorous standards, and only approved matings were permitted. Weimaraners only became more widely known during the 1940s, when the breed was introduced in the United States. Their sleek, silver-grey appearance attracts keen interest, but it is not always appreciated that Weimaraners need proper training to ensure the best development of their working abilities.

These dogs have active natures and must be able to have a good run every day. They have proved obedient and make loyal companions, while their coat needs very little attention to remain immaculate. Occasionally, a long-haired form of the Weimaraner crops up in the litters of normal dogs. These cannot be registered, but are otherwise identical to the true Weimaraner in terms of temperament.

5
GIANT BREEDS

LARGE DOGS OVER 30 in (76 cm)

These giants of the canine world are relatively few in number and, obviously, you must have adequate space to accommodate them. They can, nevertheless, prove loving, gentle and adorable companions, in spite of their size, although they will not be as long-lived as some of the small breeds.

DEERHOUND
(SCOTTISH DEERHOUND)

ORIGINS	COAT TYPE/COLOUR
Scotland	*wiry;* *dark, bluish-grey*
HEIGHT	**WEIGHT**
30 in+ (76 cm)	*85–105 lb (38.6–46.7 kg)*
CLASSIFICATION	
hound/coursing	
NATURE	
good nature; plenty of exercise required	

This is the tallest of the various mastiff breeds, and has been known for over 400 years. Its modern ancestry can be traced back to Germany, where these dogs were originally used for hunting wild boar. Here they are known as *Deutsche Dogge* and the original German standard for the breed has since received virtually universal acceptance. Brindle, fawn, blue and black varieties are all recognized, as well as a harlequin form. This is basically white with the body coloration broken by either black or blue patches, although the former coloration is favoured.

The short coat of the Great Dane is easy to keep in good condition by using a body brush.

Although they require plenty of exercise, do not be tempted to allow young puppies to run excessively before the age of six months or so, as this can cause lasting damage to the tendons and joints in the limbs. Bigger dogs in general tend to have a faster growth rate than the toy breeds, which can leave them more susceptible to problems of this type. Naturally, the Great Dane's appetite is in proportion to its size.

You may need to rearrange your house with a Great Dane puppy around, as they tend to be rather clumsy and bang into things. As a result of their size, they are not the best choice for a home with young children, although this breed is generally good-natured.

IRISH WOLFHOUND

ORIGINS	COAT TYPE/COLOUR
Ireland	*wiry;* *wide variety*
HEIGHT	**WEIGHT**
30 in+ (76 cm)	*85–105 lb (38.6–46.7 kg)*
CLASSIFICATION	
hound/coursing dog	
NATURE	
trustworthy, friendly	

Better known in North America as the Scottish Deerhound, these hounds were bred before the advent of the gun, to assist in the capture of red deer for the table. Pace and stamina were essential characteristics, and Greyhounds appear to have been involved in their early development. Changes in hunting techniques contributed to the decline of the Deerhound, but Queen Victoria helped to ensure the survival of the breed, which was immortalized in paintings by the artist Sir Edwin Landseer.

It is not a common breed today but retains support from a dedicated group of owners. Deerhounds are good-natured dogs and settle well in spacious domestic surroundings. They need plenty of exercise, and will still chase game if the opportunity presents itself. Although the Deerhound may appear somewhat similar to the Irish Wolfhound, it can be distinguished by its over-all sleeker appearance. A good brushing of its harsh wiry hair will be adequate. Dark bluish-grey is the favoured coat colour.

GREAT DANE

ORIGINS		COAT TYPE/COLOUR
Germany		*short;* *wide variety*
HEIGHT		**WEIGHT**
30 in (76 cm)		*120 lb (54.4 kg)*
CLASSIFICATION		
working/guard		
NATURE		
can be clumsy; generally good-natured		

The future of the Irish Wolfhound was in doubt during the early years of the nineteenth century once the wolves themselves had been eliminated from Ireland. The breed had been kept here for as long as 2,000 years, its ancestors being known to the Romans. The survival of these friendly giants was almost entirely due to the efforts of one man, a Scot called Captain George A Graham. Working with the few wolfhounds that were still alive in the 1860s, and using judicious crossings with Deerhounds, Graham was able to re-create this ancient breed.

Standing up to 34 in (86 cm) tall, the Irish Wolfhound is the tallest dog in the world, but, in spite of its size, it makes a trustworthy companion as well as proving an alert guard. The breed is only suitable, however, if you have a large area of land around your home where it can gallop about. As with other large breeds, long walks are not recommended for young wolfhounds, but they still need plenty of exercise. The wiry coat needs relatively little attention, and a wide range of colours is established, ranging from black through fawn, brindle and red to pure white. Puppies have to be trained from an early age, as, in view of their size, they can otherwise prove something of a handful in later life.

INDEX

Major entries, with illustrations, are indicated by
bold page numbers. Minor illustrations are
indicated by *italicised* page numbers.

PICTURE CREDITS

PHOTOGRAPHS BY MARC HENRIE: P.7 (TOP LEFT), P.8 (TOP), P.11 (BOTTOM).

ILLUSTRATIONS BY PAUL HART, KATE HARRISON AND HELEN JONES, FROM THE SCHOOL OF ILLUSTRATION, BOURNEMOUTH AND POOLE COLLEGE OF ART AND DESIGN.